Dog-Gone Murder

A Queen Bees Quilt Mystery

by

Marnette Falley

Other books in the Queen Bees series:

Murders on Elderberry Road - by Sally Goldenbaum
A Murder of Taste - by Sally Goldenbaum
Murder on a Starry Night - by Sally Goldenbaum

Dog-Gone Murder
A Queen Bees Quilt Mystery

By Marnette Falley

Editor: Doug Weaver
Cover illustration and map: Neil Nakahodo
Character illustrations: Lon Eric Craven

Copyright © 2008 The Kansas City Star Co.

Published by Kansas City Star Books.

First edition.

ISBN: 978-1-933466-71-2

Printed in the United States of America by Walsworth Publishing Co., Marceline, Missouri

To order copies, call StarInfo at (816) 234-4636 and say "BOOKS."

Order on-line at www.TheKansasCityStore.com.

STAR
BOOKS

Dog-Gone Murder

A Queen Bees Quilt Mystery

by

Marnette Falley

KANSAS CITY STAR BOOKS

STAR
BOOKS

CAST OF CHARACTERS

PORTIA (PO) PALTROW,
founder and nurturer of the
Queen Bees quilting group.
Anchors the women's quilting
group in life and in art.

KATE SIMPSON,
Po's goddaughter and
a high school teacher.
The newest member
of the Queen Bees.

PHOEBE MELLON,
wife to Jimmy, an up-and-
coming lawyer, young mother
to 4-year old twins, and a
constant surprise to
her quilting cohorts.

ELEANOR CANTERBURY,
who lives on the edge of the
college her great-grandfather founded. Is heir to the
Canterbury family fortune.

LEAH SARANDON,
professor of women's
studies at Canterbury
College. An artistic
quilter.

SELMA PARKER,
owner of Parker's Dry Goods
Store. Provides a weekly
gathering place for the
Queen Bees quilting group
and generous doses of
down-home wisdom.

SUSAN MILLER,
Selma's artistic assistant
manager in the quilt
shop. Recently returned
to college to pursue a
degree in fiber arts.

MAGGIE HELMERS,
Crestwood's favorite veterinarian. Is an avid quilter
and collector of fat lady art.

M A P

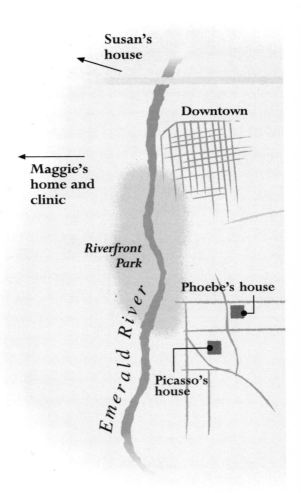

Susan's house

Downtown

Maggie's home and clinic

Riverfront Park

Emerald River

Phoebe's house

Picasso's house

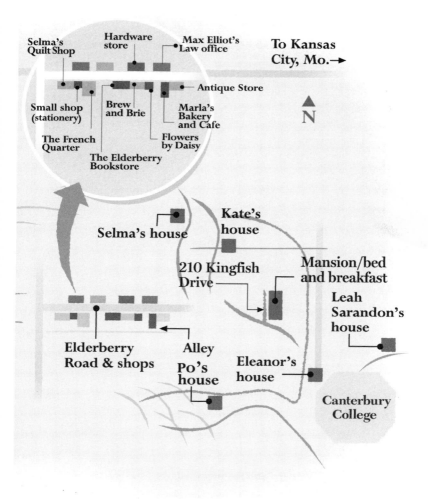

Selma's Quilt Shop
Hardware store
Max Elliot's Law office
To Kansas City, Mo.→

Antique Store

Small shop (stationery)
Brew and Brie
Marla's Bakery and Cafe

N

The French Quarter
Flowers by Daisy

The Elderberry Bookstore

Selma's house

Kate's house

210 Kingfish Drive

Mansion/bed and breakfast

Leah Sarandon's house

Elderberry Road & shops

Alley

Po's house

Eleanor's house

Canterbury College

CHAPTER 1

Po Paltrow sat on a padded wooden bench, her golden retriever, Hoover, pressed against her leg, and looked around the freshly painted clinic. "This room is beautiful, Angela," she said to the office manager as she ran her fingers against the silky smoothness of Hoover's ears. "I love those new skylights—they brighten up the whole place. The renovation was a good idea." She looked at the new magazine racks and a low, curved wall that separated the dog area from the cat side, where a young woman sat holding a sweet tabby on her lap. Several other dog owners sat in comfortable groupings of chairs, reading magazines. It was a waiting room that made waiting a treat.

Angela Carter looked up from behind the curved reception desk. She was checking appointments on the computer and keeping one eye on the young receptionist working at her side. Her ever-present smile widened when she looked at Po. "Dr. Maggie has an eye for detail," she said. "Be sure you check out the new boarding facility when you take Hoover back for his exam. It's amazing, Po. Five-star boarding, right here in Crestwood, Kansas."

Po laughed. "Well, I hear from Maggie that you're the one behind that effort."

"This is a pretty typical clinic, Po," Angela said. "It's just Dr. Maggie, and the part-time doc she hires to cover on Saturday morning and during her vacations. And Dr. Maggie's amazing. She takes care of every pet as if it were her own. But we needed a facelift badly. Folks demand more for their pets these days—some want television sets, raised beds, even heated floors. And even though it's not one of those huge practices with 10 doctors or more that you see in big cities, Helmers' Animal Clinic now has all the amenities for our boarders. Each suite even has a little camera so I can check from here to be sure all our guests are happy." Angela nodded approvingly at the receptionist as she politely finished a reminder phone call to a client.

"Well, Hoover isn't in need of television. At least not yet. He's more into chasing squirrels around my pine trees." Hoover's thick tail swept the floor at the mention of his name.

"But some clients like it," Angela said. "Take Mercedes Richardson, for example. Her Fitzgerald is much more relaxed and sleeps better with music playing and the lights kept low. He's a pointer, you know. They can be a bit high-strung if they don't get enough attention and exercise." Angela glanced at the appointment list on her computer screen. "In fact, Fitzgerald is coming in this morning for a pre-show checkup, and he'll spend the afternoon in one of the suites. We're bringing a massage therapist in to help relax him, too."

Po smiled. Fitzgerald, the only Crestwood dog to have entered the Westminster Kennel Club Dog Show, was well known in the small town for his many ribbons and trophies. His pure-bred reputation was matched only by that of his eccentric owner, Mercedes Richardson. But before Po could voice an opinion on doggie massages and heated kennel floors, the front door flew open and Champion Fitzgerald's Got It Good, the son of another champion, Fitzgerald's Miss Otis Smiles, walked in with his owner at his side.

If a dog could be haughty, Po thought, Fitzgerald was. But she had to admit he was beautiful, his coat shiny and perfect. She had heard Mercedes talk about his perfection. He certainly did have an athletic grace. His dark brown head and ears and nose did present a striking picture. And he did have it good. Perhaps he deserved to show off a bit, Po decided.

"You're right on time, as always, Mercedes," Angela said. Mercedes strode over to the counter, acknowledging Po's presence with a brief hello as she passed.

Mercedes was about 50, Po thought. She wore a suede jacket and elegant wool slacks, creased, tailored and spotless. Po wondered how she managed to stay free of dog hair. Every pair of slacks Po owned seemed determined to announce Hoover's presence in her life, even when they came straight from Herman's Dry Cleaners.

"Is Maggie ready for us?" Mercedes asked. Her tone of voice indicated that "no" was not an acceptable answer.

"She had to leave briefly on an emergency, but let me check to see if she's back," Angela said, and glanced down the hallway as an exam room door opened a crack.

Po noticed the relief on the office manager's face, imagining Maggie was in the exam room. Even though Angela had worked closely with Mercedes—helping her train Fitzgerald for the shows was her previous job—keeping Mercedes waiting for an appointment was not something she'd welcome. But before Angela could move, the door suddenly widened and a small figure raced through. Sampson, a usually sweet male cat of unknown parentage, flew down the short hallway and leapt directly onto Angela's neat desk, scattering papers in all directions.

Not to be outdone—and much to her owner's dismay—Jezebel, the three-year old tabby in the cat area, leapt from her owner's lap, across the tiled floor, and flew up on the counter, meeting Sampson head on.

Before Angela could move, the two cats were curved in perfect upside-down "U"s, their fur standing as straight as prairie grass. Hisses curled up into the air like a radiator at full steam.

Mercedes cursed and took a step back. Po leaned forward in her chair. And Hoover, head cocked, sat on alert, staring at the feuding cats, poised in a tense standoff.

Po reached down and patted his head. "It's all right, Hoover," she said quietly, "Just give them space."

A 6-year-old girl, sitting beside her mother and holding a small fluff of a puppy, screamed. On a soft cushioned chair, the owner of a Boston Terrier tensed and scooped up the small bundle of black and white onto her lap.

Angela slowly moved around the counter and looked over her shoulder.

Aaron Whitaker, his tall, lanky frame filling the examining room doorway, was ashen-faced. "Angela, I didn't mean—"

"Aaron, get me a blanket," Angela said, her steady voice cutting him off. "Now."

"What?"

"A blanket," Angela repeated. "And a broom." Her brows were pulled together but her voice stayed calm and crisp.

Aaron, at 6 foot 2 and still growing, looked baffled. Another look from Angela sent him scurrying to the cupboard.

The cats, sensing indecision, renewed their combat, hissing and spewing at one another. And in the next moment, Jezebel leapt on top of Sampson, sinking her claws deep into his back.

Sampson, in a move that rivaled ballet's Mikhail Baryshnikov, shook free, leapt off the counter, and landed directly on the back of Fitzgerald Richardson, Crestwood's one and only claim to the Westminster Dog Show. Before Fitzgerald could react, Jezebel followed.

Angela held up one hand to stop Mercedes from grabbing the cats, and with the other, she grabbed a slender can of compressed air standing beside the computer. With one swift movement, she pressed the button on the can and sent a fierce flow of air just to the side of the fractious cats, startling them into inactivity for one brief second. But it was long enough for Aaron to throw a blanket over each cat, causing them to tumble to the ground and freeing Fitzgerald. Grabbing the broom, Angela forced it between the blanket lumps to be sure the cats

cats were separated. With the help of the young receptionist and Aaron, they carefully lifted each bundle and released the cats in separate exam rooms, quickly closing the doors behind them.

"Take Fitzgerald into the exam room," Angela said to Mercedes, and Mercedes, for perhaps the first time in her 50 years of life, obeyed.

"The cats need a little time alone," Angela explained to the frightened young woman whose cat had been so peaceful just moments before. "Jezebel is still angry, but she'll calm down soon, and then we'll take her some food and check her out for bites."

"I don't know what happened, Angela," Aaron stammered. "Sampson was with me one minute, then disappeared. Geez— of all dogs to get hammered."

"Shush, Aaron. It happens. Cats can be hard to restrain." Angela half-smiled at the distraught young man, then quickly turned and hurried after Mercedes and Fitzgerald.

Aaron, his face beet red, looked over at Po. "I sure am sorry you saw that, Mrs. Paltrow. Please don't tell Kate. She got me this job."

Po smiled. "Don't worry about it, Aaron. Kate tells me you're wonderful with animals. One mistake doesn't change that."

"I like working here. Dr. Maggie is great."

"That doesn't surprise me a bit. Maggie is one of my favorite people," Po said. Maggie Helmers, the owner of the clinic and a devoted member of the Queen Bees quilting group, was also the most popular veterinarian in Crestwood, and Po knew this was a prime part-time job for Aaron, as long as he could survive the Mercedes Richardsons of the world.

And how lovely of Kate to arrange for the job, Po thought. Her goddaughter continued to surprise her at every turn. As a teenager, Kate had caused her mother, Liz, and Po no end of worry, but she had grown into a gracious, caring adult who would fill her mother to the brim with pride. It was moments like this that made Po want to pick up the phone, call her closest friend, and say, "Lizzie, get over here this instant. The martinis are chilled. We shall celebrate our Kate." But since Liz's death a few years ago, the martinis could no longer be shared. Still, Po felt instinctively that somehow the sentiment still was.

"So you like working with animals, Aaron?" she asked Kate's prodigy.

"Sure do, Mrs. Paltrow. Remember when I used to play catch with that Great Dane you had before Hoover?"

Po laughed as memories flooded her of the gigantic dog that her children rode like a pony. "Of course I remember. Dino was his name, and you were such a tot you could practically walk beneath him. "

Po remembered well those years when Aaron's mother made ends meet by cleaning houses in the Elderberry neighborhood where Po lived. She'd bring Aaron along, and he loved being in the Paltrows' large, treed backyard, playing on an old rope swing Po's husband Sam had built for their own children. But what he'd loved most was playing ball with Dino. Once Aaron started school, Po had lost track of him, though she knew his life hadn't been easy. And then he ended up in Kate's senior English class, and Po caught up on his life. With Kate's help, he'd gotten a scholarship to Canterbury College, and Kate continued to keep an eye on him, helping him get odd jobs

Dog-Gone Murder

to help make ends meet.

Aaron leaned over and scratched Hoover's head. "Well, buddy, I'm just glad those feisty cats didn't land on you." Though the front door hadn't opened, a chill fell over the threesome as Hoover's tail continued to thump on the floor, his warm eyes focused on Aaron. Po looked up.

Mercedes Richardson stood at the reception desk, ignoring the young girl behind the counter. She was staring at Aaron, her steely grey eyes piercing and cold.

"Mercedes," Po began. "How is Fitzgerald? Angela did a fine job of protecting—"

"Young man," Mercedes said, ignoring Po and filling the space between herself and Aaron with icy air.

"Ma'am," Aaron said. "I'm sorry about the cat. It got—"

"Be quiet," Mercedes said sharply. "And listen closely."

Her voice was so cold, her words so punctuated, that a chill ran up and down Po's arms. She rubbed it away, wanting to interfere, to somehow protect Aaron from the crushing force of Mercedes' words. But she was being silly. Mercedes hadn't said anything. Hadn't really done anything.

Mercedes took a step closer to Aaron then, her perfectly coiffed blond head still and her eyes never leaving Aaron's face. She raised one hand as if to slap him or punch the air, but instead, she held it in front of her chest, her fingers clutching Fitzgerald's leash and curled into a tight fist. With the other hand she pointed at Aaron's face, her finger a poison arrow, and continued to speak.

"If you ever so much as touch my dog, I shall personally see to it that you never work in this town again. You will be ruined. Ruined. Or worse. Mark my words."

And with that, Mercedes Richardson lifted her chin into the air and walked to the door. She paused for a brief moment, her hand on the brass knob, and turned back to the room. A controlled smile, focused on Po, creased her lips.

"Good-bye, Po," Mercedes said. "It was lovely to see you again." And she opened the door and walked into the warm fall day, Fitzgerald's leather leash dangling from her fingers.

CHAPTER 2

Po smiled as she watched Kate arrange on a dish the cranberry scones she'd bought down the street at Marla's Bakery and help herself to a cup of steaming coffee. It was four years since the cheery, athletic young woman had returned to town to mourn her mother and Po's best friend. At the time, she thought joining her mom's quilting group was a temporary thing. But in the end she'd never returned to her cozy apartment in Boston. "So often life doesn't run down quite the path we expect," Po thought, as she looked at the group of women that made up part of her permanent support system and smiled.

At this meeting in the back room of Selma Parker's fabric store, a weekly ritual of sewing and friendship, they'd get a glimpse of what their current project would look like finished—a quilt they would donate to the Humane Society benefit auction. Appropriately enough, veterinarian and lifelong quilter Maggie Helmers contributed the vision for this piece. And sure enough, just as Kate joined the rest of the group at the table with her warm mug, Maggie bustled in. "Does everybody have their squares done?" she asked as she dropped a full tote against one wall and filled a mug.

Their pet-themed contribution was titled "Bad Karma." It was a nine-square quilt featuring eight cats. Now it was time to see how the Queen Bees had each brought their little critter purring and scratching to life.

The Saturday morning group had met at the back of Parker's Dry Goods for as long as anyone could remember, beginning back when Selma's mother had run the store. Over time, the dynamics of the group changed with the changes in the members and their lives. But still, some of the Queen Bees were friends and relatives of the women who started this weekly tradition.

Po smiled as she looked around the room. These seven wonderful women had begun as her quilting companions, but over time their lives had become pieced together in the same way as the complicated projects they conceived and executed. She could no more imagine her life without them than imagine her days without quilting or her home without the quilts she created with them.

With Maggie's arrival and question, each Bee dug in her bag and produced a square. They laid them out in order on the giant worktable they used in the back of Selma's fabric shop. The first was clearly good-natured and sweet looking; Po could practically hear it purr. Every cat in the middle shifted a little more toward the crabby end of the cat scale, until the eighth warned you with every whisker that if you got your hands too close, you would suffer the consequences. The ninth square held a dopey-looking, floppy-eared, wide-eyed dog.

"I think it's perfect, Maggie," she said. "Nothing could appeal to pet owners more."

"I think the variety is neat," Maggie said. "I expected from the beginning that we'd all use a mix of piecing and appliqué. But there were even more decisions on the fly and problem-solving than normal with this project, I thought."

"Yeah, I bet it took everybody some fiddling to get the expressions right," agreed Phoebe, the vivacious, petite mother of 4-year-old twins. "Lucky for me, I took the easiest. My sweet kitty just smiles. That wasn't too hard."

Kate and Phoebe, the two youngest Bees, were the least experienced quilters and had the least free time. And the rest of the group was happy to accommodate their busy schedules in order to keep them around. That way they could contribute another point of view, and the joy of quilting would spread to another generation of quilters.

Two weeks before, the Bees had each chosen a cat to work on; Kate took the dog. Po had volunteered to do two. Maggie had handed each one an enlarged photocopy of her original sketch to work from. And then they'd hold what were always vivacious discussions about colors and fabrics. In the end, those initial choices would make the final project, done by eight sets of hands, feel unified and whole, like the Queen Bees themselves—more than the sum of the parts.

In Maggie's original sketch, she had used only brilliant blue and vibrant orange to outline her eight cats and the dog who filled the final square, and the Bees had talked about following through with that first impulse. In the end, however, they agreed you could stray, if needed to make the expression you were going for work. "But," said Susan, one of the newer addition to the Bees. Her acknowledged expertise in color and ongoing studies in fiber arts often gave her the last word in these discussions. "Let's make these color voices dominant," she said.

Then they'd chosen six fabrics that would represent the color palette for the piece, and each Bee took a fat quarter. That way, they'd likely have some of the same fabrics in every square. And they'd each have a palette to mix on, as it were, when they chose complementary textiles to paint with.

With the finished squares laid out on the table, they were finalizing their decisions about the binding and sashing. "Perhaps black and white?" Susan suggested. "Or maybe a deep navy? What do you think of these?" and she laid a couple of additional bolts of fabric on the table.

As they talked, a tall, dark-haired young man burst in at the back door of the store, looking shaken, and out of place. "Aaron!" said Maggie. "What's wrong?"

"Fitzgerald has disappeared, Dr. Maggie," he said. "You have to come right away."

Not two minutes later the strained young man and the Bees' project leader were gone, leaving the women agape and almost speechless.

"I was there at the same time as Mercedes two days ago when she dropped Fitzgerald off at Maggie's clinic," Po said finally. "She was in rare form."

"Maggie has told me about the list of special instructions her team gets when Mercedes boards the dog," said Kate. "She wants them to wash his linens every day, but no fabric softener. At least three walks and two outdoor play periods, but only playtime with the dogs she's approved."

"I know she's wildly proud of that dog," said Leah. "But it does seem a little intense." Leah was a professor at Canterbury College. And Po secretly thought that if Leah thought it was intense, that was a real sign. Leah was extremely creative, and yet could be very structured. She had to be to manage all those students and their work. And the combination made her a strong contributor for the Queen Bees. But still. The criticism was sharpest coming from her.

"He did win Best in Breed at Westminster a few years ago," Selma said. "I remember there was a huge write-up in the paper." Selma Parker owned Parker's Dry Goods, an anchor for the Elderberry Road area for more than 50 years—and the weekly meeting spot for the Bees.

"And if you missed that, Mercedes will remind you," Phoebe said. "She manages to work that in almost every time I see her at the country club. She could stand to cut back on the caffeine a bit; things might go better for her."

Po laughed. She had come to count on Phoebe to contribute

irreverent comments on all the goings on around her. And Phoebe hardly ever disappointed her.

Wild-child Phoebe's straight-laced in-laws maintained her membership at the country club and quietly insisted that she find occasion to use it. Adoration for her up-and-coming lawyer husband and a strong desire to have her beloved babies grow up in a sphere of family harmony ensured her compliance, but it wasn't always an easy road. In her words, the high society circles her in-laws cherished featured "too many prunes and not enough piercings."

"Fitzgerald's care gets particular focus, but I've heard she's the same way about everything," Eleanor said. At 85, the well-connected heir to the Canterbury fortune knew almost everybody—and often quite a lot about them. Her great-grandfather had settled his family along the banks of the Emerald River more than a century ago. He'd found the perfect place to build a thriving fur trading business. And with his other life ambitions achieved, he decided the town needed a college. So he built one in his own backyard. Eleanor lived in the elegant family home, separated from the campus by one elegant wrought-iron fence. And for all those years, the family had been in the know.

"Yeah," Phoebe chimed back in. "I've seen her order her own food at Picasso's, and it's got as many requirements and a don't-mess-with-royalty, kiss-my-hem attitude that just won't stop. I don't know how anyone could live with her. Nothing is ever good enough. Even Picasso's!"

Conversation died for a moment, as each of the Bees contemplated the joys of Picasso's menu at The French Quarter, a restaurant just two doors down, and wondered how anyone could find fault with the delicacies the jovial chef concocted. Po's very favorite meal there was still Picasso's steaming bouillabaisse and a loaf of crusty French bread. It made her mouth water to think of it now.

"She's married, though. Remember?" Leah said. "And for a while now."

"That's right," Eleanor said. "It was kind of a to-do at the time. Mercedes has some family money, and she married her handyman."

"When was that?" Po asked. "About 10 years ago?"

"Maybe 15," Eleanor said.

"Pretty decent deal for him, huh?" said Phoebe. "Maybe he still does some of her handyman work, but it can't be that bad to have just one client. Although he does have to live with her dog."

"Make that dogs," Po said. "I think she's actually got six or seven."

"Well, I take it all back then," Phoebe said. "Taking care of Mercedes' seven dogs on top of actually living with Mercedes seems like anything but the lap of luxury."

About that time, the store got busy, and Selma and Susan helped quilters pick out their new projects, found the perfect complement to that fabric they dug out of a closet, and consulted on yardages. Before long, Po found herself standing alone with Kate just inside the heavy wooden door that led to the street.

"Kate," Po said slowly. "I didn't want to say before, but Mercedes seemed particularly angry with Aaron when I was

Dog-Gone Murder

at the clinic. She made a big scene, and told your young man not to go anywhere near her dog.'"

"You're kidding!" Kate said. "I've found Aaron so dependable. In fact, I recommended him to Maggie."

"He told me that," Po said. "And hopefully, it's nothing to worry about. But Mercedes was mad enough to want him fired when she thought he was careless about letting the cat out. It makes me worry about what she'll do if she thinks Aaron has played any part in the dog's disappearance."

"I'm glad you mentioned it," Kate said, pushing the door open with determination. "I think I'd better watch out for that boy—and for Maggie." Maggie and Kate had known each other since the now-doctor started babysitting her younger neighbor some 30 years before. And the renewal of their friendship since Kate had returned to Crestwood was wonderful for both of them.

"Now, don't be rash," Po warned as Kate tossed back her unruly mane of hair and corralled her project supplies on her bike rack. "It may all be fine."

"Or it may be nothing but trouble, Po," Kate said. As she headed out, she released the handlebar to wave at her dear godmother—and Po felt a dark sense of foreboding.

"I'm sure I'm overreacting," she thought as she slung the tote where she'd stashed the fabric she'd bought for the binding. Selma and Susan had offered to piece this week, and she'd said she'd do the binding when they got to that.

Just seconds after she headed for her car, she saw something that make her think her misgivings might be well grounded: the proud shape of Mercedes Richardson emerging from the office of lawyer Max Elliot across the street.

"What could she be talking to Max about?" thought Po.

C H A P T E R 3

Po had tossed her new fabrics in the washer and was working on her own quilt project. An experiment for her, she'd started by painting on silk. Now she was using that sunset smeared swath of nubby, hand-dyed silk as the background for a gnarled tree branch. Usually, she found the inspiration of meeting with the other Queen Bees was just what she needed to fuel a productive day. But today, the disruption of their meeting and the worry she felt for Maggie left her staring at the display wall she used to track her progress.

"This is crazy," she said to herself. But her small nudge of anxiety didn't go away. So she picked up the phone.

"Hi, Max," she said when his warm voice answered. "I know we were planning to have a quiet evening, but would you mind if I invited a few other people over?"

Po's frequent companion laughed. "It's Saturday. I really didn't think you'd be able to hold the group size down. Go ahead and plan your party."

"Max?" Po continued. "Did Mercedes come see you today? I thought I saw her car at your office when I was leaving Selma's shop."

"She did stop by," Max said. "I work with her on her estate planning."

"Is she good to work with?" Po asked.

"No worse than the worst," Max said with a laugh. "But then, you know, as a lawyer, I don't generally see people at their very best. They don't want to talk about the stuff attorneys talk to them about."

Po laughed. "Good thing you're not my attorney, I guess." With invitations left for Kate and Maggie to have a drink and to grill, Po felt calmer. Satisfied for the moment, she sat down at her beloved Bernina and lost herself in the warm whirr of the machine, the changing landscape of pattern and color, and the flashing needle.

Around 5, Po opened the door and found Kate on the doorstep with a bottle of wine in one hand and a fruit pie in the other. "I did a little hunting and gathering on the way over," she said.

"You're a dear, Kate," Po said. And moments later, Po handed her a glass of the chardonnay she had already chilled, put the bottle Kate brought into the fridge, and shepherded her goddaughter out onto the giant deck. Then she put the final touches on a tray of cheese and fruit and popped some artichoke dip in the oven. She poured herself a glass of wine just as she heard Maggie's clunker of a truck pull into the driveway.

Maggie had been threatening to get rid of her rattletrap truck for years. Every time she found herself under the hood coaxing it to start, in fact. But she never actually made the move. She did often show up with streaks of dirt or oil along one side of her arm or on her cheek. And she did tonight.

Po smiled when she saw the proof that the truck was still acting up, and handed Maggie a tissue. Just a minute later she and Maggie joined Kate in the peaceful, treed backyard. There was a soft evening wind blowing, and a quiet rustle of fall leaves moved in the background.

"What a day," Maggie said, sinking into one of the many available chairs.

"Poor girls," said Po, looking at the clearly exhausted Maggie and Kate. "So, give me an update. Did you figure out how Fitzgerald got out?"

"All I can think is that the electricians let him out," Maggie said, sighing. "They were doing the last work in the boarding area, getting the Web cams and the new TVs set up."

"Was Fitzgerald in one of the suites?" Po asked.

"Yes," Maggie said. "He was in the tropical getaway suite. Mercedes is one reason I finally decided to take on the addition. As difficult as she can be, she's our top client. And she was talking about taking all her dogs somewhere else for

Dog-Gone Murder

boarding. And she's not the only one. My clients tend to see their pets as members of the family. They sure don't sleep on a concrete floor at home."

Po looked at Hoover, who was lying, as normal, at her feet. The tray of snacks was clearly holding his full attention. It was true she had three dog beds in the house for him: one in her room, one in her quilting studio and one in the sitting room. Not that he slept there if the sofa was unguarded, she thought.

"The problem," Maggie continued, "is that the workers swear he was there safe and sound when they left. But he sure wasn't there when Aaron went to walk him this morning."

"Of course, none of this is going to matter to Mercedes," chimed in Kate.

"You mean she doesn't know?" Po said.

"We haven't been able to get a hold of her," said Maggie. "Angela called every number we have, with no luck."

"Wouldn't it be great if you found Fitzgerald before she called back," Kate said a bit wistfully.

"Boy, it'd be a lot better than it's going to be the way things stand," Maggie said. "We've done everything we can think of. We called the shelter and all the other veterinary clinics in town. We drove all over town looking for him. We made a flier and posted 500 copies." She trailed off.

"Aaron is still out looking," said Kate. "He's still feeling bad about letting the cat get away from him yesterday. Even when all the rest of us gave up for the day, he refused to quit. I think he took Mercedes' dressing down very personally. He's trying to redeem himself. But he's maybe overdoing it."

"Oh, the dip," Po said, jumping up and heading for the kitchen. As she pulled it out of the oven, brown and bubbling and smelling of parmesan, she heard a quick knock, and local lawyer and terrific martini mixer Max Elliot let himself in. "You know, you should lock that door," he said, pulling Po to him for a quick hug and his characteristic warm, just-for-her smile.

Po often thought no one could replace Sam, her late husband. She still missed having that partner in her life who shared more than 30 years of her history. But that didn't lessen her appreciation for this gentle, modest man who watched out for her and kept life interesting.

"Yes," she said, with an answering smile. "I know."

"Don't you say that every time you come in?" asked Kate, who'd come in for a refill.

"Yes," he laughed. "Someday maybe she'll listen." Max made himself a drink and joined the group around the snacks. Maggie and Kate got him up to date on the events of the day, while Po started the grill and put together a salad. She was just about to put the kabobs on the grill when Maggie's cell phone chirped.

"Man, I hope it's good news," she said, stepping inside to take the call. But when she came back out, they could see from her tight shoulders and firmly set lips that it wasn't.

"Oh, Maggie," said Kate. "Clearly they didn't find Fitzgerald yet."

"No," Maggie said looking as worried as they'd ever seen her. "And as predicted, Mercedes doesn't care how hard we're trying."

"What did she say, Maggie?" Po asked, with concern clear in her voice.

"She's threatening to sue me," Maggie said, with tears filling her eyes. "She told me that she'd sue me for Fitzgerald's future winnings and for the lost value of his future offspring. And she said she's calling the local television station and the newspaper tonight to tell them how careless we were."

"That is so unfair," Kate burst out. "Your team has been so dedicated to finding him. And you don't even know how he got out."

"I knew she'd be beside herself," Maggie said. "I've been waiting all day for her to find out and the bomb to hit. But if the paper picks it up, the story really could kill my business.

"You know, Mercedes hasn't actually been in herself as often lately," Maggie said. "More often her son-in-law, Jack Francis, has brought the dogs." She paused. "Bad luck really, that she happened to be there when the cat attacked Fitzgerald. I'm sure she's adding that relatively minor aggravation to this more serious problem."

Maggie paused.

"What is it, Maggie?" Po asked gently. "Is there something else going on?"

"Well …" she hesitated another long moment as she looked around the table at her friends.

"I can't figure it out," she said finally. "But the practice isn't doing that well."

"What do you mean?" said Max with a thoughtful frown. "That seems impossible. Don't you fill up your appointments pretty easily?"

"We're superbusy," Maggie said. "But we're not making enough. If Mercedes really does sue me, I could go out of business."

Max kept probing. "Is this a new problem?" he asked.

"Well, I've had times when the going's been rough before," Maggie said. "When I started the clinic, for sure. And when I first really hired help. More salaries sure make a huge difference; I had to learn to work more efficiently. But I've had some time in the middle where everything seemed fine."

She paused again.

"It's embarrassing, you know," she said. "I feel like I should know my own business well enough to have all the answers. But I'm afraid I feel way more comfortable with a difficult diagnosis than I do with a cash-flow problem. I've been just hoping that things would turn around. Now it looks like I don't have time for that."

"You know we'll do anything we can to help you," said Kate with feeling.

"We absolutely will," said Po.

Max was still thoughtful. "Who does your bookkeeping, Maggie? Do you think he or she could help you think through your revenue issue?"

"Oh Max, I don't know," she said. "Jane Flemming does it for me. But she just manages the payroll and does my taxes. Today I'm not sure I even care about the other issues. I've mostly been thinking about it when the truck threatens to break down. But what would I do if I lost my practice? It's everything to me. I swear, Mercedes doesn't care about anyone but herself. She's about to kill me, and she's not even going to lose a minute's sleep."

Maggie looked so distraught, none of her friends had the heart to push her for more answers about anything, even after they'd all finished their roast beef and Po's classic salad. She almost always used a basic vinaigrette, a mix of high-quality olive oil, garlic salt and balsamic vinegar that she'd pour together over the salad without ever measuring. Sometimes she'd mix in some Dijon mustard, when she felt in the mood for a little extra zing. The result was consistently delicious.

"It's all going to be fine, Maggie," Kate said with certainty as she cleared the plates after the main course. "We'll make sure of it."

And with that declaration, they'd all finished off the apricot pie and said their goodnights. The two younger Queen Bees drooped, they were so tired after the emotional events of the day.

Even with the worries Maggie faced, she went to sleep right away—although she slept fitfully. But Po and Max spent awhile talking after they left about how they could help. And when she finally went to sleep herself, Po had an action plan prepared. Step one would commence at breakfast.

CHAPTER 4

Po got up early and went for a short run. Since the days when her kids were old enough to get themselves up on school days she'd sneaked out of the house quietly in the first light of the day to breathe in the crisp air and the sweet smells and enjoy what was often the only solitude in her day. Now for more than 20 years she'd been repetitively setting one foot in front of the other, and her treks through the small college town she called home gave her nothing but peace. She felt such serenity—and her travels down those same roads again and again gave her opportunities to be grateful for the time she'd spent raising her family in Crestwood, building a rich network of friends and living a life that she always enjoyed. She had considered moving when her dear Sam died. Her sister had extolled the virtues of living in Florida at a point when it seemed her world was falling apart. But she was glad she'd stayed where their family's roots had sprouted.

Of course, the regular exercise also meant she could wear the flattering classic clothes she liked and still indulge in her favorite social engagements, which all involved food. Like the evening on the deck before. And the breakfast to come, post-run, at Marla's Bakery.

For more years than she liked to tally, Po had met Leah Sarandon for omelets or scrambled eggs or sinful eggs Benedict on Sunday morning, a tradition born of their husbands' lack of interest in eggs and love of early-morning golf. They discussed whatever book roused their always-vivid interest and imaginings, the progress or problem of the latest quilting project, and whatever else came up.

Leah's contacts on campus, developed from 15 years as a professor of women's studies, coupled with Po's deep ties in the community, meant they often heard two different sides— or three or four—of the same story. Marla's broad circle and unabashed enthusiasm for sharing information also helped keep the two in the know about local goings-on.

"It's not a bad place to start the search for solutions," thought Po as she walked in, thinking, as she had been almost without stop, about Maggie's concerns about her clinic and the prized pooch who disappeared from there.

She lingered by the door, waiting for her friend and enjoying the warm smell of baked goods and rich coffee. Before she knew it, she saw Leah striding her way, her long skirt flowing around her boots and her arms swinging in her tailored leather jacket. Po thought, as she had hundreds of times before, how much she admired Leah's strong personal style.

The bakery was hopping, and Marla didn't have time to do anything but wave when they walked up to request a table. And once they were seated in one of the dark green booths— Po always preferred a booth to the small round tables—one of the wait staff filled their coffee cups, a sign that Marla was finally yielding to the growth her shop experienced and delegating some of the work. She simply could not take every order, fill every cup, and scrub down the tables and green-and-white tile floor every day all by herself. Although she tried. Tableside was, after all, the best place to learn what was happening in town. And she found the gossip at least as sustaining as the food she loved. Maybe more.

With weighty, confidential issues on her mind, Po was a little relieved to find herself in a table near the picture window, a long way from the kitchen, and with enough chatter around them to cover the conversation. Since the night before she had wanted to talk with Leah about the dog's continued disappearance and Mercedes' legal threat.

She just managed to let Leah start her coffee, and then she brought her up to speed on the previous day's events. It wasn't until the heavily laden plates arrived—eggs Benedict for Po and a rich quiche for Leah—that Po paused for breath.

"So, they haven't found Fitzgerald yet?" Leah asked.

"I'm sure Maggie would have called if they had," Po said. "And boy, that would have been great news to wake up to this morning."

Dog-Gone Murder

"I have to think the electrician let the dog out," Leah said thoughtfully. "But I think John Cline is working on that job. And he is so reliable. He's done all kinds of work for me. The last job was my upstairs bath, remember? That was last year. I gave him my key, and he came and went. I just can't believe he wouldn't say if he'd made a mistake."

Po clearly remembered the bath. It had started as an old, traditional, small bath. Leah had gutted the room, taken over a closet from the guest bedroom next door, and transformed the space with a mix of bold color and clean white tiles and vintage fixtures. Leah was the only person Po knew who successfully mixed and matched dramatically colored towels. And plates. And chairs. It was a gift.

"How well do you know Mercedes?" Po asked.

"I really don't know her well," Leah replied thoughtfully. "I did have her daughter in class once."

"What was she like?" Po asked.

"Gosh, that had to be more than five years ago. Mostly I remember her boyfriend waiting for her outside like clockwork. And I saw later that they got married."

Just then Marla bustled up, unable to resist the temptation to chat with her longtime customers. "Hi, quilters. Staying busy with all your projects? And who got married?" she asked, curiosity, as always, getting the better of any slight instinct toward discretion.

"We were talking about Melanie, Mercedes Richardson's daughter," Leah replied patiently. It had long been a source of irritation to the Queen Bees that Marla so regularly insinuated that they spent "soo much" time (clearly she thought "too much") on such an "old-fashioned" hobby.

"Oh, right. She and Jack Francis have been married for about four years, I think," said Marla, thinking. "In fact, they were here yesterday. And they didn't look that happy. I wonder if they're having trouble."

Now her voice dropped very low, and she looked around to see who was listening—a clear sign they were getting the juicy scoop now. "In fact," she said. "Daisy Sample told me he canceled his regular flower order."

She looked around again.

"That man sent his wife and his mother-in-law flowers every week for years. Until now."

"Really?" Po said, despite herself. She really did try not to encourage Marla.

"Yes, really. And this morning, he and Melanie hardly said a word to each other."

"Well, that's hardly conclusive," said Leah. "They may just be watching their budget a little more. Flowers once a week is pretty lavish."

"Well, but Mercedes has lots of money," rejoined Marla. "I've heard Melanie always got whatever she wanted. And Jack Francis has that dealership."

"Really?" Po said again.

"Yes, the one out on Highway 32," she said. "He sells classic cars. You know how he always drives that flashy red Pontiac GTO around town."

The conversation was making Po think she hadn't been paying enough attention to the various doings of Mercedes and her family. Or to the cars she saw around town. "Hmm," she finally said with a smile. "I guess vehicle identification isn't really my strong suit."

Leah laughed. "I can't imagine," she teased.

Over the course of the breakfast, the conversation turned to other topics, as it always did. The books they were reading. The new line of fabric they'd seen. Their progress on pet projects. But Po's mind never entirely gave up chewing on the mysterious disappearance of a cherished champion from Maggie's clinic. And Leah knew it was still on her mind.

"So, what do you think, Po?" Leah asked when they found themselves with the bill paid and out on the curb.

"Complicated question," Po said, with a smile. "I think we need to find the dog. Mercedes is perfectly capable of suing dear Maggie. And I think we need to pretend to buy a car. I'm interested in Jack. Maybe he had a reason to steal Fitzgerald."

"I never considered that the dog might be stolen," Leah said.

"Well, I guess I think we need to start thinking that way," Po said.

"OK, then," Leah said. "You go to Maggie's, and I'll go to the dealership."

"Sounds good," said Po. "I just need to stop by Selma's. Then I'll go. But don't go to the dealership by yourself," she said. "Take Kate. She might even like looking at the cars. She used to drive a cute little car in high school. I can't remember what kind. I do remember her mother was always worried about her driving too fast."

Leah smiled. "OK," she said. "I'll try to track her down."

"And then come for dinner and report," Po said. "We'll do something easy. Are you free?"

"What could be more pressing?" Leah asked. And with that, they each headed off.

CHAPTER 5

Po walked down the street six doors to Selma's. When she'd made her cats for the benefit quilt, she'd made four extra. She wanted to make them into a little wall hanging. In fact, she always tried to make a memento for herself when they tackled a group project. When she saw these small pieces, she remembered the fun they'd had and the events they'd discussed during the project. Each one was oddly like a photo album or a scrapbook for her, it recalled so much.

She had been so distracted by the abrupt end of their meeting on Saturday that she hadn't had time to think about what she needed to finish that smaller piece. She wanted a calm moment to wander around the store. When she was really ready to start something, she sometimes felt as if the right fabric would jump out and claim her. It was worth a walk through to see whether that kind of inspiration was at the ready. Even if it wasn't, she needed some deep forest-green thread for her other project. So the trip wouldn't be lost either way.

She sighed gently when she walked into the fabric store. It always gave her a sense of possibility and a calm peace to see all the fabrics arranged by color and materials.

She was just admiring a particularly bright batik in the window, a strong purple piece with a bright orange-and-white pattern, when she saw Mercedes' husband, Jarrod Richardson, walk by. She was tempted to duck at first, dreading an overflow of anger given Fitzgerald's uncertain whereabouts. But then she saw he clearly hadn't noticed her. Why would he? They had only met a couple of times; he replaced her garbage disposal more than a decade ago. And he'd been very nice. He really wouldn't expect her to know anything about the missing dog, either, she thought when her moment of panic had subsided.

And then she noticed that he seemed anything but angry or distraught. In fact, he seemed to have his head in the clouds. He strode through the Sunday morning passersby, intent on their coffees and strolls, with a smile and a bounce in his step.

"Interesting," Po mused as she watched him walk up the street. And then she returned to the rack of fabric and the decision at hand. "I really never go wrong with purple ..." she murmured, and she was lost to the thought. At least for a little while.

She carried her final choices to Susan at the cutting table.

"With all the excitement yesterday, I had to come back to think about what else I might need," Po said.

"Poor Maggie," Susan said. "I'm sure she is so worried."

"You haven't heard anything, have you?" Po asked.

"No," Susan shook her head.

"I tell you what, though," Susan said. "I've been wishing I could do something. I'm thinking I might stop on the way home and walk part of the river. It would be super long odds, but imagine if I found him."

"That would sure be fabulous," Po agreed.

"And at least that gives me something to do that could help," Susan went on. "That always makes me feel better."

Po left Selma's with a yard of the purple batik; a subtle tan and white plaid that would contrast dramatically; a half a yard of each of the fabrics the group had originally chosen to work in; her forest-green thread; and the enthusiasm for a new project that she always got when she started to hold bolts of fabric together and imagine the final product. As she pushed open the door, she stopped for a moment and eyed the building across the street, wondering what Max was up to. His car was there, she saw.

Making a mental note to call him later, she walked out to her car, feeling relatively upbeat about her plan to head for Maggie's clinic. Then she saw Jarrod suddenly emerge from the hardware store, on the other side of the street. Po hesitated, and then shut her door again and walked across the way to meet him. As she did, she thought, as always, what a handsome man he was. And it's true, his unruly hair and tall, fit frame made him a striking figure.

"Hi, Jarrod," she said. "I'm Portia Paltrow."

"Of course," he said with a ready smile. "How are you?"

"Oh, I'm fine," she said. "I heard that Fitzgerald is missing, though. I wanted to say how sorry I am. He hasn't been found, has he?"

"No, I'm afraid not," he said, his deep brown eyes clouding over a bit. "Mercedes is fit to be tied. She's worrying about everything from whether to withdraw from the dog show next month to whether to cancel his grooming appointment tomorrow."

"I feel so bad for her," Po said. "I know how I'd feel if my dog were missing."

"Well, I'm going to go look for him some more this afternoon," Jarrod said. And then he suddenly smiled. "And don't tell anyone," he said with a conspiratory look, "but I'm going to sneak in a little fishing while I'm out by the river. I just picked up some bait." He nodded back at the hardware store, and Po remembered vaguely that there was a fishing section in the back corner.

"What are you fishing for?" she asked.

"Catfish," he said with a wide smile. "But next weekend I'm hoping to go to the lake and fish for trout. I bought some new lures, too. Trout season opened this week, and I'm hoping for an opportunity to go enjoy it."

She smiled. "Well, that's making the best of it, I'd say. I hope he turns up soon."

"You and me both," agreed Jarrod, loading the sack he was carrying into the back of his SUV. And with that he was on his way.

Po took the bridge over the river, admiring the view as she always did. The nights had just gotten cool enough to start turning the maple trees and the sumac to their rich fall orange and red, and Po thought again how nice it was to have the beautiful autumn colors and still be enjoying such sunny warm days. She pulled out of her reverie and into the drive of Helmers' Animal Clinic in fewer than 10 minutes.

Po smiled to see Maggie's name on the prominent new sign. She knew Angela had really twisted her arm to get it. Po agreed with the office manager. The sign, with a stone base and a lovely planting of blooming mums below it, complemented the new entrance to the clinic beautifully. The enhanced visibility and name recognition was worth the fight against the practitioner's natural modesty. And business seemed to be booming. And yet…

Po put aside her troubled thoughts and pushed through the front door.

"Hi Po," Angela greeted her with a smile. "Where's Hoover today?"

Po walked up to the counter, smiling at the warm receptionist.

"Oh, he's probably napping on the sofa," Po laughed. "A dog's life. Slight jealousy on my part is the natural state of things."

"Do you need food?" Angela asked clicking a few buttons on the keyboard in front of her to find Hoover's record. "Hoover eats the senior diet, right?"

"You are so organized," Po said with a smile. "You're right; I should pick up a bag of food. But really, I came to check in on Maggie." She looked around the waiting room, to make sure she wouldn't be overheard. "There's no news about Fitzgerald is there?" she asked quietly.

"No, I'm afraid not," Angela said with a worried look. "Aaron's been out looking again all morning." She leaned in even closer. "And Mercedes called me last night. She was really angry. Maybe as angry as I've ever seen her, and that's saying something. We just have to find Fitzgerald." Angela suddenly stopped.

"Didn't Maggie tell me you helped train him?" Po asked.

"Yeah," Angela said with a small smile. "I've even shown him for Mercedes. I've been too busy here in the last year or so, so she's been working with someone else. But he's a great dog." Her forehead wrinkled again. "I'm worried," she admitted. "And not just for Fitzgerald. Mercedes could really cause Dr. Maggie a lot of trouble."

Angela broke off suddenly as the door pushed open. "Hi, Mrs. Johnson," she said. "I'll be right with you and Betsy." Betsy was a black miniature poodle with a pink "princess" collar and a cocky canine smile. And for the millionth time, Po was struck by Angela's gift at remembering people and helping to build the bonds of Maggie's clinic. She really did make it pleasant to visit. And she knew Angela had lifted a huge burden off Maggie in the time since she'd joined the practice, handling lots of day-to-day management so Maggie could focus on caring for pets, her mission since she was just a child.

Angela turned back to Po. "Dr. Maggie should have a few minutes while Tess starts talking to Mrs. Johnson about

Betsy's history. Will that be enough for you to talk with her?"

"That will be great, Angela," Po said. "Thank you."

Angela showed her to Maggie's small office, and sure enough, moments later Maggie dropped into her office chair, looked over the desk at her friend and sighed, wilting into a heap. "Hi, Po."

"Is there anything I can do, Maggie? I've been wishing I could help you today."

"I sure appreciate it, but I can't think of anything." Maggie looked worried and tired. She rubbed the back of her neck unconsciously, ruffling the curls at the base of her head. Po would bet money that she'd spent most of the night awake.

"Maggie," she said quietly. "I know you've been thinking that Fitzgerald escaped. But is there any reason someone would take him on purpose?"

Maggie's eyes widened. "I never considered that," she said, surprised. "He's a valuable dog, but you couldn't show or breed him without giving yourself away."

"Really," she mused, "he's more valuable to Mercedes than to anyone else."

"Taking Fitzgerald would certainly be a blow to Mercedes then, right?" Po said.

"Well, yes, that's true," Maggie said. "But if someone took him, they'd have to get into the clinic to do it. That's a little scary."

"You really haven't even looked for signs that someone broke in, though, have you?" Po asked.

"No, we haven't," Maggie agreed. "But I think we'd have noticed anything obvious." She paused for a moment, thoughtful.

Dog-Gone Murder

"Still," she said, "right now more people than normal would have access. We've had electricians and plumbers and contractors and painters and who knows who else troop through in the past three months to do the work on the reception area and build the boarding suites. They don't all have keys, but some do. And we've left them here in the evenings to close up after themselves."

Just then Angela stuck her head around the doorframe. "I'm sorry to interrupt," she said, preparing to back out.

"It's OK, Angela," Maggie said. "What do you need?" She came in, looked at Po, and then perched on the edge of one of the two chairs in Maggie's office.

"You know I don't like to get anyone in trouble," she said.

"Of course," Maggie said. "What's going on?" Angela sat for a few seconds, looking at her feet.

"I think Aaron might be stealing food," she said.

"Really?" Maggie said, sounding surprised.

"I didn't want to think so," Angela said, her words tumbling out in a hurry now. "He's so nice. He always pitches in and he's great with the dogs and all. He never complains. But this is the second time I saw him load a big bag in his trunk."

"Do you know when exactly?" Maggie asked. "On what days?"

"This weekend was the second time," Angela said. "On Saturday. And the first time was about a month ago, but I don't know exactly."

"I appreciate you bringing this up," Maggie said. "I'll meet with him to discuss it."

"You won't tell him it was me, will you?" Angela said.

"I don't want him to be mad with me."

"I'll try not to bring you into it," Maggie said.

"Thank you," Angela said. "I really do think he's a good guy."

And with a tight smile, she stepped out and left the two friends looking at one another.

"One more problem," Maggie said. "Just what I need."

"Do you really think he took the food?" Po asked.

"There's no way to know without talking with him," Maggie said. "And then it still may not be a sure thing."

Maggie stood up and smiled wearily at Po. "I hope I come out of this one, Po."

"We'll figure it out, Maggie," Po said with more confidence than she was feeling. "Do you mind if I look around a little before I leave? And can you come for dinner tonight? It won't be late, I promise."

Maggie smiled, gave her permission to snoop, promised to come by later and disappeared into the exam room next door to tend to little Betsy.

Po left Maggie's office feeling a little unsure of her next step. What exactly was she going to look at? As she stood in the hall uncertainly, Angela bustled by.

"Are you heading back out, Po?" she asked.

"Actually, I thought I'd take a look around," she said.

"Really?" Angela stopped short. "What are you looking for?"

"Well..." Po felt funny sharing her motivation, but how would she learn anything if she didn't start asking a few questions. "Well, it occurred to me that maybe someone let Fitzgerald out on purpose."

Angela looked shocked. "But… but…" she stuttered for a moment. "Who would ever do that? And why?" she said.

"Well, I'm not sure," Po admitted. "Maybe it's a crazy idea. But still, I thought I'd take a look around, just in case." Angela was still staring at her mutely.

"You haven't noticed anything odd, have you?" Po persisted.

"No," Angela said. "Although we've been in a bit of an uproar, what with our team being scattered around looking for Fitzgerald."

"Well," Po said. "I think I'll at least take a close look at all the doors. And could you give me a list of everyone who has a key?"

"Well, of course," Angela said, regaining something close to her normal composure. "I'll do that for you right now. I actually had to make some extra keys recently, to give to the contractor. But I can easily make a list of who has them," and with that she headed back to the front desk.

Po remembered that there was a side door to the clinic. Maggie had suggested that she leave that way on the difficult day when they'd put Moppin to sleep. A black Lab, Moppin had followed her young children all over the house, cleaning up any little spills they'd made. When she'd stopped eating, they knew the then-old dog was really ready to move on. But that hadn't made the decision any easier.

At least she'd had Maggie, Po thought. Maggie really understood how important Moppin was to their family and how much they'd miss her. And for how long. Maggie's team had sent her a single red rose after their sad visit and a card where they'd all shared their memories of her sweet pup.

But it was Maggie who'd checked in over the next few weeks to see how she was doing. And it was Maggie who understood the worst moments. When she woke up at night from a dream in which Moppin had nosed her and found she was gone. When she walked into the house and noticed for the 50th time that it was lacking the greeting she'd come to expect over 12 years with her four-legged girly. And it was Maggie who shared her joy when Hoover presented himself and made it clear that her house and her heart were intended all along to be his one day.

Po made the short walk down the hall, past the comfort room that Maggie and her team used for special visits, including complicated conversations about pets and their owners' options, such as euthanasia. And, just as she remembered, she found the door to the outside, where bereaved pet owners escape so they don't have to face a reception area full of cheery dog and cat owners. The door had a keypad, which she assumed went to an alarm. She opened it and examined the doorknob, but didn't see anything unusual. Feeling a little foolish and slightly let down, she went looking for the back-door.

"Can I help you?" asked a young woman as Po wound her way to the less public area of the clinic. Po had only been through the treatment area once before, during her first tour.

"I'm a friend of Dr. Maggie's," she said with a smile. "Could you show me the back door? I'm doing a little unofficial snooping about Fitzgerald's disappearance."

"Oh, sure," said the slight blonde, with an engaging smile.

"I'm Catie. I started here about six months ago. Come this way," and she headed down the hall.

"I mostly clean the kennels. I know it sounds like a drag, but it's so fun to be with the animals," she trailed off. "Here you go."

The back door looked just like the one on the side, the same grey metal. The same keypad.

"Do you each have a code?" Po asked.

"Yes," Catie confirmed. "I was super afraid at first that I'd set off the alarm and the cops would come, but so far so good," and she laughed.

Po opened the door and examined the lock outside. Again, nothing. She noticed a relatively large enclosure to the left of the door, at the bottom of the two steps down to the alley. "Is that the trash?" she asked Catie.

"Uh huh," Catie said. "And also the freezer."

"Freezer?" Po queried.

"Well, many pet owners have their pets cremated when they die," Catie said. "But if they don't choose to cremate their pet, we put the bodies in the freezer."

"Really?" Po said. "Then the owners bury them?" she asked.

"Sometimes," Catie said. "But in some municipalities it's not allowed. And some pets never get claimed. Our refuse service takes away anything we tag in the freezer when they pick up the trash.

Po decided she was glad she'd had Moppin cremated.

"Well," she said. "I guess that's it."

"I sure hope you figure out where Fitzgerald is," Catie said earnestly as she walked Po back to the front of the hospital.

"He really is a beautiful dog."

"Aren't they all?" thought Po as she walked back to the front of the clinic. And she vowed to take some time after she ran to the store and before she started dinner to throw Hoover his favorite tennis ball and brush him down. "At least 20 minutes," she thought.

She stopped back by the front desk where Angela had a bag of food and the list of people who had keys and codes to the clinic waiting. Digging through her purse, Po paid with the cash she'd picked up during her Saturday morning banking. Moments later she was headed to her car with the list of people who had access, the spot-on medication that kept Hoover victorious in the battle against fleas, and the uncomfortable feeling that there must be something more to learn.

CHAPTER 6

Hoover lay panting on the rug when the doorbell summoned Po. She found Maggie beaming on the front step in the shade of her 75-year-old oak tree and flourishing a bottle of champagne. "We found Fitzgerald!" she said the instant Po opened the door.

"That's wonderful news," Po said with relief. "Oh, I'm so thrilled. Who found him?"

Maggie stepped into the house and headed to the kitchen with Po in tow to put the bottle in the fridge where it would stay cold. "Aaron found him on his last pass down by the river," Maggie said. "Angela called just a few minutes ago to tell me. He took Fitzgerald back to the clinic and gave him a bath. They said he doesn't look as though there's anything wrong with him." Maggie looked at her watch. "I wanted to go check him out myself, but Angela said she'd already called Mercedes. She didn't want to deliver him late, after all this trouble." Maggie shook her head. "And it's sure true that none of us needs to face any more of Mercedes' wrath. Anyway, Aaron's probably on his way to Mercedes' house right now."

"That is such wonderful news," Po said again. "Everyone will be so pleased."

"I'm working on an appropriate toast for when the rest of the crew gets here," Maggie said. "Right now all I can think is, 'Thank God!!'"

Po laughed. "I certainly think that will work," she said. Moments later Kate and Leah let themselves in and learned the good news.

They poured the champagne and toasted to Fitzgerald and friendship, and then they gathered on the back deck again to eat some hummus and cut veggies and get the details while they waited for Max, who was coming just a little later. It was getting a bit chilly in the evenings, so Po had laid a fire in the chiminea and had passed out sweaters that she kept near the back door for these occasions. No one was surprised. They knew Po extended the out-on-the-deck season as far as she could.

Kate was always sitting just as close to the fire as she could get. And it was a ritual with her to wash the campfire smell out of her hair when she got home from Po's.

"I guess we don't need to give our report now," said Kate with an exaggerated sigh. "Darn, because we did such a good job."

"We still don't really know how Fitzgerald got out, though," said Po thoughtfully. "Of course, it may not matter so much now that he's back. But it would still be nice to know what happened. Maybe we do need the report."

"Oh," said Kate. "True. OK." She paused for a moment and looked at Leah.

"Well, we went by the dealership. I pretended to be looking for a car, and I asked for advice. They had a really darling blue Mustang, but I told him I had my heart set on red. The killer part is that I used to own one. I should never have gotten rid of that car."

"Your mom was pretty happy when you did," Po said with a laugh. "She was always worried you'd land in a ditch in the winter."

Kate laughed at the memory of her mom's many lectures on the topic. The thought emerged as a throaty rumble. Kate's laugh always made Po smile, too. Although she often thought that Kate's laugh always seemed too big for the space around her, somehow.

"It's true that they're not that great when it's slick and icy," Kate said. "That's why I keep driving my sensible junker and riding a bike. When I start thinking about my dream cars, I need about three. A Jeep for the snow. A convertible for the summer. A monster truck so I could pull a boat to my as-yet-only-imagined lake cabin. I can't afford the insurance on my fleet. And it would look ridiculous when I parked them all in front of my house. In fact, I doubt there's enough curb."

Leah smiled. "You seemed pretty interested in the idea of a red Mustang today, for sure. You were very convincing."

"I'm easily enthused," Kate said. "One of my most charming qualities, I'm sure. Anyway, the sales guy went to check on what else they'd have coming in."

"That was great," Leah chimed in, "because we learned that Jack Francis wasn't there. He came back and said he wasn't sure, but that his boss would be back in the morning, and he might know about other cars that would be available over the next three to six months."

"Leah worked magic here," Kate said. "She asked a bunch of questions about how many cars they get in and whether interest seems to be accelerating."

"It does seem from the answers that the dealership may be in trouble," Leah said. "He said there might not be anything for a while—but that he could make us a deal on something in stock. He seemed pretty anxious to sell us something."

"It's hard to know whether that's unusual, though," Kate admitted. "I sort of expect car salesmen to wheel and deal, you know?"

There was a pause as they all thought about what Kate and Leah had said. Then, with his usual impeccable timing, Max arrived to fill the gap in conversation. He topped off all their drinks and got himself one. They toasted to Fitzgerald's good health and got Max up to date on his whereabouts. Then they talked about the quilt for the benefit, celebrating their progress to date while Po bustled around getting dinner ready. She had made lasagna with Italian sausage, one of Max's many favorites. She slid some bread into the oven to warm and tossed the salad with her traditional oil and vinegar dressing. In just a few minutes they gathered at her long table to eat.

"Do you know Jack Francis?" Po asked Max as they all started helping themselves to the available fare.

"Not really," Max said. "I've met him a couple of times, but only because I've done some work for Mercedes."

"What did you do for her, Max?" Kate asked.

"I consulted with her on her estate planning," Max said.

"So you know who gets what?" Kate asked.

"Yes," Max said with a smile, "but you know I can't tell."

"Isn't that always the way," said Maggie with a laugh. "You never get to tell the good stuff."

Po wanted to ask some more about Mercedes, but she dropped it, for the moment. She knew Max didn't like to talk about his clients' business. But maybe there was something he could tell her later that would help.

In the meantime the conversation shifted. Kate got some advice from Leah on her next week's class. Maggie and Kate made plans to go to an interesting exhibit at a nearby art gallery.

Leah left the gathering first, anxious to tackle the first stack of papers she'd received from this semester of students. "I am not getting behind this year," she vowed as she made her goodbyes, "I have my personal Teacher of the Year award picked out, and I intend to earn it."

Leah picked out a piece of jewelry at the beginning of the school year, and then she'd buy it on the day she turned in her grades to celebrate the successes of her year. Po thought it was an inspired idea. She always asked about it, and Leah took her by her favorite jewelry store to point out the necklace she'd picked out. It was a five-strand freshwater pearl necklace, with spacers of peridot, and aquamarine. It would look stunning on Leah, Po was convinced.

Kate headed out next. She was meeting P.J. Flannigan after he got off his shift. Her tumultuous first love from high school had provided the same excitement and a warmer friendship since they'd become reacquainted on her return to her hometown. When he wasn't on duty, you could generally find the handsome police officer with Kate. "Is P.J. off on Friday?" Po asked. "It seems like forever since he's come by."

"I'll ask him," said Kate with a knowing smile. She knew Po watched over their deepening relationship with the mix of affection and anxiety that her mother would have felt. "You know you're his favorite meddlesome aunt ever," she teased. Po just smiled. She actually was god-mother to both Kate and P.J., although she was never certain whether they'd made that connection.

Maggie and Max were putting away the leftovers and washing the dishes when she rejoined them.

"I can do that," Po protested.

"But so can we," Maggie said.

Po smiled, and gave up the fight as she had so many times before.

"Would either of you like a cup of coffee?" she asked.

"No, I've really got to get running," Maggie said. "I'm just beat. I haven't been sleeping well. And now that we found

Fitzgerald, I know I'm going to sleep the sleep of the dead," She smiled. "I'm due, I think."

"Maggie," said Max. "Have you thought any more about calling that consultant I suggested?"

"I have thought about it," Maggie said. "I have to admit, I'm a little uncomfortable having someone pry through my business affairs."

Max smiled. "I did think you seemed a little hesitant." She wrinkled up her face. "Well, what if it's bad news. Maybe I don't want to know."

Po put a hand on her arm. "It's just the next thing, Maggie. You'll figure it out."

"I could give her a call and introduce you," Max offered. "Would that help?"

"Oh, Max, you're the best," Maggie said. "That would be great."

And with cordial goodnights all around and a roar of her old truck, the good-natured pet doctor was gone.

"You are the best," Po said with a smile up at Max. "Thank you for helping her."

"If it makes you happy, it makes me happy," Max said, giving her a gentle squeeze.

CHAPTER 7

Po went to sleep that night thinking that they'd dodged a bullet. That feeling lasted through most of the day. She drank her coffee and enjoyed the paper. She pulled her new fabric out of the dryer, and spent some time looking at the sketches of tree branches and leaves she'd made over the past couple of months, cutting out bits of fabric, and trying to clarify her vision for the piece she was working on. And after lunch, she worked on researching an article for Fabric Artist, a piece that focused on new techniques for fusing. And all the normalcy of her day disappeared in one instant when she picked up the phone and heard Maggie's distraught voice.

"Oh, Po," was all she got out, and Po could tell that she'd celebrated too soon.

"What happened Maggie?"

"The police have been here," Maggie said in a strangled voice. "Mercedes has disappeared."

"You're kidding," Po said. "How can that be?"

"I don't know," Maggie said. "But they found her car, apparently abandoned. It looks like she never came home last night. And she missed her appointments today."

"Well, that all does seem unlike her," Po said.

"The worst part is that her family seems to think we had something to do with it. They sent the police to Aaron's apartment this morning to ask him who was there when he dropped Fitzgerald off. And they just left the clinic. They came to ask me about the dog disappearing." She trailed off.

"I don't know what to do, Po. What should I do?"

Po's mind was whirring. And she knew Maggie's was, too. So her first bit of advice was really not that helpful. And she knew it.

"Don't worry, Maggie," she said. "We'll figure it out." But what to do wasn't coming easily. "You go back to work," Po said. "Let me think about it. Do you think you can get away early today? We can regroup then."

Maggie said she'd try to reschedule her last couple of appointments for the day, and that barring that, she'd call the veterinarian who covered for her when she went on vacation. And with that she ran off to adjust her day, leaving Po to adjust her thinking from "all's well" to "all's tumbling." And, of course, to start working on a plan.

Information gathering is always the first step, she decided. So she placed a call to Kate. She felt a little bad, asking Kate to prod P.J. for information. But, she figured, what's the good of having an in with the Police Department if you can't use it in an emergency? Po had caught her on her planning period, time she spent grading papers and planning lessons. Kate promised to make the call right away.

With that job assigned, Po called Phoebe. She smiled, as always, to hear the twins in the background. At 4 years old, the identical blond boys showed all the enthusiasm for life that their mother did, which made them tough to keep up with. Despite the challenges of getting a free evening away from her cherubs, Phoebe agreed to go with her mother–in–law to her weekly Women's Club meeting at the country club on Wednesday night to see whether she could learn anything from Mercedes' crowd.

Then Po called Maggie back, and left her a message, asking whether she could bring Aaron along. It seems like he might have noticed something that could help.

And then she made a shopping list. "After all," she thought. "We can't possibly do any creative problem solving on an empty stomach." And with that she headed to Elderberry Road.

Her first stop was at Picasso's restaurant, The French Quarter. It wasn't the first time the amiable restaurateur had put together a range of hors d'oeuvres to go for Po. Her combined love of company, Picasso's cooking, and food that comes in bite-sized pieces made it a terrific arrangement.

"My dearest Po," the round, starched-apron-wearing

Dog-Gone Murder

French chef said, smiling broadly when he saw her. "What a pleasure, as always. You look as beautiful as ever. To what do I owe the pleasure?"

Po smiled. "I'm hoping you can indulge me again, Picasso. Would you be willing to prepare five or six appetizers to go? I'm going to have four or five guests this evening."

"Of course … having a party?" he inquired jovially.

"Not exactly," Po said. "Maggie is in some trouble, Picasso. Mercedes Richardson seems to be missing, and the police have questioned Maggie and her team."

Picasso's face fell. The year before, he had been suspected of the murder of his wife. So he knew the trauma of being involved in an investigation firsthand.

"That is big trouble," he said with a frown. "And that Mercedes is not very nice. She is never happy with her food."

"When was the last time she was in, Picasso?" Po asked.

"It has been a while since I've seen her," Picasso said. "Her husband comes now and then. Like you, he asks for 'to go.'" He shrugged. "You Americans and this 'to go' thing," he said with a smile and a snap of his thick fingers. "Everything quick."

Po laughed. "I promise to come back and luxuriate in eating another time," she said. "There's nothing better—really. But today, I'm going to be a speed-demon American."

She arranged to pick up the appetizers in half an hour, and set off for her next stop.

Marla was not at the bakery, so she escaped quickly with a loaf of fresh baked sourdough. Just five minutes after she left Picasso, she was standing at the checkout with Ambrose

Sweet in Brew and Brie with two bottles of her favorite merlot. Ambrose and Jesse co-owned the wine bar, and Po wished it were Jesse working. She knew him better, and enjoyed his dry wit.

Ambrose finished checking out the young woman in front of Po—she'd picked a Chianti—and turned to her with a smile. "Hi, Po," he said. He looked around quickly to make sure none of the browsers was listening before he dropped his voice and continued. "Hey, I heard that Dr. Maggie found the missing dog, but that now the owner is gone."

Po nodded. "Yes, I'm afraid that's true," she said slowly.

"Well, I got it from a pretty reliable source," he said. "And nothing about it's going to be good," he said, shaking his head. "That family can be dogged," he half-smiled. "Not a good thing, but punny, given the circumstances."

"Really," said Po noncommittally. "What makes you say that?"

"Well, you know Mercedes," he said. "She gets her way whether she's bullying the City Council about the ordinance she wants passed or lobbying her local store owner for a better price on brie." He shrugged. "Blood relative or not, that son-in-law of hers seems to have inherited the same stubborn streak."

"I don't know him well," said Po.

"Well, I don't exactly run in his circles," Ambrose said. "But from what I hear when he hits a fight-or-flight situation, the choice is always fight. He's a bulldog, whether you're talking a golf game or a hunting trip, is what I hear. He has to win and has to be right. Too bad that bullheaded approach doesn't translate to success in business."

"Is his dealership not doing well?" Po asked.

"It's not like I see his numbers, or anything," Ambrose said. "But I sure know he has trouble keeping a sales team. Jesse has some friends at the other dealerships around here who hire the good people away. And when you don't have team players, you have to watch your back every second. It's hardly possible to win in the long run."

He handed Po her receipt. "I'm glad you're looking out for Dr. Maggie, Po," he said. "I think someone needs to with that clan in the mix."

Po knew the store owner meant well and his undercurrent of warning left her with a pit in her stomach that she didn't think her provisions would fill. Not even the tower of treats that Picasso had ready.

With supplies laid in, Po found herself home, ready for company and with an hour to spare before she could reasonably expect anyone to show up with more information. Unable to focus on anything else, she pulled out the list of people who had the keys or codes to enter Maggie's clinic.

She was so deep in thought, the ring of the doorbell made her jump. And the normally pleasant sound of visitors arriving sounded somehow discordant.

It was Maggie. "Aaron said he'd come by, too," she said. "He had class, but it gets out at four. So he should be here in an hour or so."

Maggie followed Po back to her study, where Po started stacking up the things she'd been working on.

"Oh," she said. "Wow, I love your other cats."

Po had the extra cats she'd made sitting out to help her think through her wall quilt. She was assigned the meanest-looking when they divvied them up, and he had quite the snarl, a line of sharp teeth and a scowl that made it clear that this feline was not one that would respond that well to an outstretched hand and a 'here, sweet kitty kitty.' Her other cat had been sort of in the middle of the mix, and Po had created an elegant, feminine, sleek cat who seemed to look at you with one eye over one shoulder. She'd made two each of those. One for the group quilt and one for her smaller wall hanging. Then she'd experimented with a couple of other ideas to fill out her little set. One was a bit abstract, with an eye that seemed somehow separate from the rest of his face. The fourth landed securely in the sweet arena, if still somewhat on the artistic side.

"It was so fun to see how you all made my rough idea real," Maggie said. She turned to Po with the first real smile of the day. "The quilt's going to be great, isn't it."

"Hopefully the auction will earn a lot for the humane society," Po said as she stacked up her fabrics and picked up thread and scraps from around her sewing table.

"They really do need it," Maggie said, looking now at Po's sketches and at the other partly finished pieces of cats she had started cutting out and then discarded. "They desperately need to make some improvements to their facility."

"There's just a couple of weeks left now," Po said. "So good thing we started when we did. We'll need to really keep moving to get it done on time."

"Selma's a gem to work on the piecing this week," Maggie said. "And then Susan said she'd clear her schedule to do the quilting." She paused. "Boy, do I owe them." Then she renewed her tour of Po's ongoing work.

"Oooo, this is great," she said, moving to the display wall. Po had felted the longest wall in her studio, which gave her somewhere to hang works in progress—an invaluable solution, Po thought, for her "thinking it through" stage of creation.

The piece that Maggie was looking at clearly arose from a botanical muse—all different kinds of leaves hung from a branch that was made of millions of scraps of fabric, bound together in a swath of silvery gray netting. "I'm experimenting," Po said with a smile.

"That's why I love to come by your house," Maggie said. "You're always experimenting. It's so fun to see what you're working on."

The sound of the door swinging open and Kate's cheery call of greeting brought them back to the entry, and after a round of greetings they headed to the heart of Po's house, the enormous kitchen. Kate stacked some small logs in Po's fireplace and expertly coaxed a warm flame into being while Maggie poured the wine and Po finished transferring the goodies Picasso had packaged up for her onto a tray.

"Mmm," Kate said as she peeked around Po's shoulder to see what she was doing. "Yum and more yum. What all do you have there?"

"Picasso is taking care of us this evening," Po said. And indeed he had.

She generally asked him to just put together whatever he thought would be good. And her reward today was a package of thinly sliced Genoa salami, shaved prosciutto, sliced Havarti cheese, roasted nuts, and a salad of marinated Roma tomatoes and garlic stuffed green olives. Served up with slices of fresh bread from Marla's bakery, it was a feast. Given that all three women had been running around preparing for this afternoon discussion, the food was just the fuel they needed.

They sat for a moment and took the first few sips of wine and bites of food in mostly silence, savoring the moment and the respite from the worry and thinking of the day. And then Maggie sighed.

Po turned to her. "So," she said. "Tell us what exactly happened at the clinic this morning."

"Well," Maggie said. "Angela and I were there early. We normally open at 7:30. I was there at 7 to check the pets that had stayed with us overnight. Everything was fine. Ellie Johnson and Max had the first appointment of the day. When I came out of the exam room at about 8 a.m. there were two officers talking to Angela at the front desk."

"You poor thing," Kate said. "How stressful."

"I really couldn't imagine what they wanted," Maggie said, inhaling the rich, round smell of her wine. "We went to my office and they started to ask questions. They asked about Fitzgerald disappearing, about how we found him, about whether Mercedes had threatened me or anyone on my staff, about when Aaron returned the dog, about whether he had been behaving oddly. It seemed like 100 questions."

"Did they explain why they were asking?" Po asked.

"They said that Mercedes was reported missing. And they said they'd found her car abandoned, but they didn't say where," Maggie said. "They also said that they'd questioned Aaron."

"How is Aaron doing?" Kate asked, the worry for her former student clear in her voice. "That had to be unnerving for him."

"I called him right after they left, and he seemed reasonably calm," Maggie said. "But still, I'd be upset if I were him."

"He apparently went to class today anyway," Maggie said, helping herself to a thick slice of bread and a spoonful of the spicy tomato and olive salad. "That seems like a good sign. I just feel bad for him. I don't think he's got much of a support group."

"Really?" Po said.

"Well," Kate continued. "His mom and dad divorced when he was young, and the dad never seemed to be on the scene. I think the two of them did fine, but she remarried last year and moved to Florida with her new husband. He chose to stay here and start school at Canterbury College."

"He has been very dependable at the clinic," Maggie said. "I know he needs the money, but all college students do—but they don't all show up on time."

"He was always reliable at school, too," Kate said. "That's why I recommended him to you, Maggie. I hate to see him in trouble."

"You don't really think anyone would believe he had something to do with Mercedes disappearing, do you?" Po said.

"The police knocking on his door before 7 a.m. is not a good sign, Po," Kate responded. "And Mercedes was threatening Aaron just last week, remember."

"Worse yet, lots of people know about it," Maggie said. "Remember, the reception area was full of people when we had the cat fight and Mercedes melted down and shook her finger in Aaron's face. That's one reason he was so desperate to help find Fitzgerald. She was angry with us already, and he felt like it was his fault."

"He did find the dog," said Po. "It seems like that should put some points in the plus column for him."

"Not if the police think he took the dog in the first place," Kate said grimly. "And right now, no one knows how Fitzgerald got out or where he was for two days. There's nothing to prove that Aaron didn't hide him somewhere to get back at Mercedes."

"She'd have certainly believed that," Maggie said with a frown.

"And her family has probably had a good week of hearing all about Aaron's terrible behavior and your carelessness," Kate said. "So they're predisposed to think Aaron had something to do with the dog's hiatus. In their minds, Mercedes' disappearance could easily be linked."

"What if it actually is linked?" Po asked.

"It seems like that would be bad news," Maggie said, looking serious. "Really bad news."

CHAPTER 8

Maggie and Kate looked at Po wide-eyed.

"Do you think they really could be?" Maggie asked. "I keep thinking that Fitzgerald's disappearance was just an accident."

"But if it wasn't," Kate picked up. "If it wasn't, then it would completely make sense that the two were related."

"And that's clearly what the police think," Po said. "Or they wouldn't be starting their investigation with Maggie and Aaron."

"I sure wish they'd started somewhere else," Maggie said.

"Did you get to talk with P.J., Kate?" Po asked.

"Just long enough to ask him to call when he gets off,"

Kate said. "So for now, I don't know any more."

"Well, let's think about where else we're going to start," Po said. "Ideas?"

"They're the same ideas I had when I was trying to think about who might have taken Fitzgerald," Maggie said. "And I probably don't have enough of them."

"We've got to start somewhere," Kate said.

"Well, we've got the lead that perhaps Jack Francis and Melanie are short on money," Po said thoughtfully. "Leah and I heard that from Marla—remember the canceled flower order? And we've got some confirmation from Ambrose at Brew and Brie and also from your reconnaissance at the dealership, right, Kate?"

"Yeah, I think that's fair," Kate said. "But how does that help us? Fitzgerald disappearing doesn't help Mercedes' family's finances, does it? And Mercedes disappearing seems to hurt them, too. No?"

"Well, they actually have quite a pack of dogs," Maggie said. "I see them all for routine care. I think there are eight. And eight dogs bring a lot of expense. Especially at this level."

"Like how much?" Po asked.

"I'd hate to guess," Maggie said. "But Mercedes is for sure my biggest client. And dog food for eight big dogs is substantial. I could look up the general costs of dog ownership and start to give you an idea. And then you have to tack on the additional costs of these dogs."

"Because they're show dogs, you mean?" asked Kate.

"Exactly," Maggie said. "Mercedes always has a trainer

working with them. Usually, but not always, that person will also show the dog or dogs. You have additional grooming costs. And travel costs. And the entry fees. And sheesh, if you breed a bitch with a champion dog, that will cost you for sure."

Po looked down at Hoover, who, true to form, was lying across her feet. "Makes you look like a bargain, doesn't it." He obligingly opened one eye at the sound of her voice and closed it again, when it was clear she didn't require anything more.

"So, what we're saying is that cutting back your team by one dog doesn't save you much," Po said.

"Right," said Maggie. "Plus if you were going to get rid of a dog, it wouldn't be Fitzgerald. Of all the dogs they own, he may have the highest earning potential."

"But if you got out of the dog business entirely, you could potentially save a bunch of money, right?" asked Kate.

"Yes, I think so," Maggie said. "But really, most people don't do it for gain. They love dogs and love the breed and love the spectacle of shows. They do it because they like it."

"But," said Po thoughtfully, "it's Mercedes who loves it. Maybe the rest of the family isn't so keen."

"Could be," Kate agreed. "We might be able to find that out. Whether Jarrod Richardson and Jack Francis supported the dog show scene."

"Angela said she used to train and show Fitzgerald," Po said. "I bet she knows more about the family dynamics."

"That's right," Maggie said. "I'll ask her about it."

Dog-Gone Murder

"Would you mind if I listened in?" Po asked. "I'd like to hear what she says."

"Sure," Maggie said. "Why don't you just come by the clinic in the morning."

"Do you know why she quit working for Mercedes?" Po asked.

"No, not really," Maggie said. "She did get busier at the clinic, I think. But I never really asked. We can talk to her about it tomorrow though."

Just as she finished her sentence, the doorbell rang again, and Po opened the door to find lanky Aaron Whitaker on her doorstep, looking tired and a bit uncomfortable.

"Hi, Mrs. Paltrow," Aaron said.

"Thanks for coming by, Aaron," she said. "Maggie and Kate are here, too."

They made their way back to the comfortable cluster of sofa and chairs where the trio had settled earlier. The two-sided fireplace separated the seating from the kitchen, and a huge, rustic coffee table gave them an ample platform for their small plates and glasses. Aaron settled on a Coke, and armed with a small plateful of food, he somewhat hesitantly joined them by sliding his large frame into a large leather club chair.

Kate glanced at the other two and then took the lead.

"So, Aaron," she said. "What a mess. I couldn't believe it when I heard the police had questioned Maggie today. And then I heard they'd come by your place, too."

She paused, and Aaron nodded.

Kate hesitated, thinking about how to go on.

"Well," she said, "we're a little worried that they think you or Maggie had something to do with Fitzgerald disappearing—and now it seems Mercedes is gone, they think the two incidents are related. Is that what it seems like to you?"

Aaron's face looked a little pinched. "But I just wanted to help," he said. "I know Mrs. Richardson was all mad about that day with the cat. And then her ritzy dog disappeared. I knew she'd be furious."

"You were great, Aaron," Maggie said. "I appreciated your help looking for Fitzgerald. And you found him, which was awesome. But it looks like we might be running into more trouble." Now Maggie looked worried, too. "We need to do anything we can to head it off."

She made an effort to smile at Aaron, whose upset showed through more clearly now. "I don't need anymore trouble. And you don't either, right?"

He managed a ghost of a smile.

"What exactly were the police asking about when they came by?" Po asked. "Maybe that will give us ideas."

"Well, they asked about how Fitzgerald could have gotten out and where I found him and when. I told them I'd looked in the same places before. I just got lucky. But I'm not sure they believed me."

He paused, and Po nodded at him to go on.

"I told them someone had him tied up for a while. He had the end of a rope tied around his neck."

"Interesting," Po said. "But he was loose when you found him?"

"Yes," Aaron confirmed.

"Then what?" Maggie asked.

"Then they asked all about what happened when I took him back to Mercedes' house."

"What happened?" Maggie asked.

"Nothing," Aaron said a touch impatiently. "I didn't see anybody. I don't think there was anyone home.

"I called the clinic when I found him," Aaron said. "Luckily Angela was there. I took him in, and we gave him a bath. And then she called Mercedes and you to say we found him."

Maggie nodded. "I got the call from Angela. I wanted to go straight to the clinic to give Fitz a once over, but Angela convinced me he was fine. She and Aaron had given him a bath, and she said Mercedes was expecting Aaron to bring Fitz by. She didn't think it was worth the delay at that point." Maggie smiled. "I'm sure she was right," she said. "She always is. I had to do something to burn off my excitement a little, though. So I went to buy champagne and I came over," she said with a nod at Po.

"Mercedes said she'd come right home to meet me. And · she said that if I was there first, I should put Fitzgerald in the house. She said she'd left the back door open. So that's what I did."

"You didn't see anyone?" Kate asked.

"No. There was no one home," Aaron said. "I knocked. No answer. The door was open, and I stuck Fitzgerald inside."

"Did the police ask you about anything else?" Po asked.

He hesitated.

"They asked me not to leave town," he said.

He hesitated again.

"What is it?" Kate asked.

"They said they'd checked with the neighbors and I was in there too long for my story to be true," Aaron said.

"How long were you there?" Maggie asked.

"Not long," Aaron said, looking defiant. "But I did go in." He stopped and looked at all of them, then his words came out all in a tumble. "Fitz walked through a muddy puddle on the way to the door, and I just couldn't let him get yuck all over the floor and get in trouble again. Not after everything. And we worked so hard to find him. That was supposed to make everything better. But she's got these white tile floors...." He trailed off.

"So you cleaned up his feet and wiped up the floor?" Po asked gently.

He nodded.

"And did you tell the police all that?" Kate asked.

Aaron nodded again. "Like I said," he said. "I'm not sure they believed me."

He looked at three women, and suddenly they saw his face get firm. "I'm sick of this," he said fiercely. "And those guys are wrong if they think they can intimidate me. I didn't do anything wrong." In that moment, Aaron looked twice as big and 10 times as intimidating as any of them had ever seen him.

"Well, we believe you," Maggie said firmly.

"And we'll get it all figured out, too," Po said. "You don't have to worry."

"Thanks," Aaron said, but he looked somehow older than he had when Po'd seen him at the clinic. And there was a certain stiffness in his gait as he left, which made Po think that they'd really only seen the crest of what was a much deeper wave of anger.

"Do you think we made him feel at all better?" Maggie asked after he left. "Poor kid. Can you imagine how he's feeling? And none of this is his fault."

"I've certainly never seen him react to anything with that kind of fire before, so he's really worried," Kate said. "And we know he's innocent, but apparently not everyone does. It is so maddening to think that the police questioned Aaron today. That means that if Mercedes really is missing, they're talking to the wrong people!" Kate gave her often-unruly hair a toss over her shoulder, a characteristic "I'm taking action" gesture from the tall young woman. "P.J. will be off in an hour or so. I'll see if I can learn anything else."

Maggie followed Kate out, thanking Po as she went. "See you in the morning."

When they'd gone, Po thought over everything they'd talked about. Aaron could clearly be fiercer than she'd realized. And one other thought bothered her. When Aaron dropped off Fitzgerald, no one was home. So, where were they? "It seems like Mercedes would have dropped everything," she thought. "I wonder what could have held her up?"

CHAPTER 9

When Po woke up, her thoughts turned immediately toward her plans for the day, starting with another trip to Maggie's clinic to talk with Angela. When Maggie had arrived the day before, Po had been studying the list Angela had given her of people who had access to the clinic during the time that Fitzgerald had escaped or been stolen. "I have to admit, I'm leaning toward stolen," Po muttered to herself as she drank a quick cup of coffee and eyed the list that was still stacked on the table.

Thirty minutes later, she headed back out, dressed in a comfortable pair of cocoa pants and a brown-flecked black turtleneck. And when she arrived at Helmers' Animal Clinic, she found Maggie in her office, poring over a set of spreadsheets.

"The month-end reports," Maggie said with a grimace. "Thank goodness for Angela. I can barely get these out of the computer without her. And that consultant Max set me up with is coming tomorrow. What terrible timing." She shook her head. "Still, I have to do something. I am just barely keeping this place out of the red."

"I'm sorry, Maggie," Po said with sympathy. "I know that's got to be frustrating. And not what you need on top of these other problems."

"You're telling me," Maggie said. "And yes, wildly frustrating. We're so busy. It seems impossible that we're not making money." She sighed. "I'm sure it will all work out. It always does. And anyway, that's tomorrow's problem." She managed a wan smile.

"Good thinking," Po said. 'Today's problems today; tomorrow's problems tomorrow."

Maggie laughed. "Otherwise I might not make it," she said. "I've always had this theory. I can handle any problem if it comes on its own. Problems a la carte — no problem. Earnings are down. That's a taco. A dog disappeared. Side of beans. My employee is suspected of kidnapping. A big burrito with cheese sauce. But all of it together gives me indigestion."

Po laughed. "Genius," she said. "We'll just deal with appetizers today. Those are my favorite anyway."

She grew serious again. "Before we talk with Angela, can you look at this list with me, Maggie?"

"Sure," Maggie said. "What is it?"

"This is the list that Angela gave me of the people who have codes to get in," Po said. She spread it on Maggie's desk, and the two of them looked at the lists.

"First of all," Po said, "is there anyone missing?" Maggie thought for a second.

"I see everyone on the team here," she said running her finger down the list. "And the plumber, electrician and contractor."

She paused. "Of course, there's no way to know if any of the people on this list brought someone along or gave the code to someone else."

"That's true," Po said thoughtfully. "But I'm not sure what to do about that. I think we'll just have to go with this until we learn something different."

"How are you thinking the list can help," Maggie asked.

"Well, if it's OK with you, I guess I'm thinking I should talk with everyone on the list. It's probably a waste of time, but it's one of the only concrete steps I can think to take."

"I appreciate that you're trying to help, Po," Maggie said. "Of course, you can talk to anyone you want."

"Do you mind letting everyone on your team know?" Po asked. "I don't want to make them feel uncomfortable. Then maybe I could come back tomorrow."

"Of course I can talk with them," Maggie said. "We get together for a few minutes every morning to make sure we're on the same page about the patients we've got and look at the schedule for the day. I'll mention to them that you'll be around." She grimaced again. "And I'll remind them that the consultant will be here." She sighed.

"You really are not looking forward to that, are you," Po said.

"No," Maggie admitted. She gave Po a small smile. "I know I should be. I need the problems fixed. But I know there's a problem. And I hate for other people to know."

She smiled again. "Silly, I know."

"It's not silly," Po said. "And you'll be fine."

"Oh, I know," Maggie said. "In fact, getting some advice could set me up to enjoy my practice even more. But still ..." Just then Angela came in.

"I asked Julie to cover the front desk and Tess is backing up on the phones," she said. "Mrs. Linder called and said she can't make it, so we actually have a little breathing room this morning."

"That sounds perfect," Maggie said. "Thanks, Angela. I wouldn't be stopping to talk about this, but we're thinking maybe the disappearance of Fitzgerald and Mercedes' disappearance could be related."

"Really?" said Angela, looking surprised.

"Well, that seems like the only thing that makes sense," Maggie said. "Why else would the police come here first?"

"So, Mercedes is missing for sure?" Angela asked.

"We don't know a lot about it," Po said. "We're trying to learn more. But the police did come here yesterday to talk to Maggie. And they'd only do that if they thought there were a connection, I think."

"You know me, Dr. Maggie. If I can help I will," Angela said. Maggie smiled. "Yes," she said. "I know."

"We're wondering if you could tell us more about the time you spent training Fitzgerald," Po said. "If we can learn more about who might have taken Fitzgerald, maybe we'll learn more about where Mercedes can be."

"I can't imagine who would want to hurt Fitzgerald," Angela said. "He really is a wonderful dog."

"I was more thinking that having Fitzgerald missing might hurt Mercedes," Po said. "She really does seem attached to him."

"I think just in the way you're attached to Hoover," Angela said with a smile. "Our pets can have a very special place in our lives, can't they."

"What about Jarrod?" Maggie asked. "Is he just as fond of Fitzgerald as Mercedes is?"

Angela hesitated a moment. "I'm not sure he was exactly," she said finally. "I mean, he liked Fitzgerald fine, I think. But it's a lot of work to have eight dogs. And that was the last count at Mercedes' house. Of course, some of them are just fostered. They go away eventually. But many are theirs, and the dogs are getting training, and eating and needing exercise. It's a lot of work."

"Who took over the training when you cut back?" Maggie asked.

"Oh, it's Samantha Herron," Angela said. "She's very nice. She works with lots of dogs, and has done it for ages. Fitzgerald was in good hands." Angela got very serious. "I really couldn't have quit if I hadn't been sure that someone great would be stepping in. But I knew she'd do a great job."

"Why did you decide to quite training him?" Po asked.

"I just got busier. I was starting to work more hours here," she said, "and that made it harder to give him the time he needed. And I got tired of the travel."

"Did you have to travel much?" Po asked.

"It was quite a bit," Angela said. "To get enough points to be considered for Westminster, a serious owner wants you to be showing almost every weekend."

"That must have been stressful," Po said.

"Now that he's not showing as much, it's an easier job. I'm sure Samantha is loving it," Angela said.

"Does she take care of the other animals, too?" Po asked.

"Yes, I'm sure she works with all of them at least a little," Angela said. "But still, there's lots of work left over for the rest of the family."

She dropped her voice and leaned a little closer. "The truth is, I thought Jarrod was about done with the dogs when I moved on. I just don't think he can change much about what Mercedes does. Especially not when she's got her heart set on it. And Jack Francis was always complaining about the money they cost."

"Jack Francis and Melanie live with Mercedes and Jarrod, right?" Maggie asked.

"Yes," Angela confirmed. "But it's a huge place. Jack Francis and Melanie have their own wing, bigger than most people's houses."

"But why would Jack Francis care what Mercedes spends on her dogs? It's her money," Maggie said.

"This really isn't very nice to say, but I think he's been counting his inheritance since the day he got married,"

Angela said. "And in his eyes, she's spending it."

"But it sounds like she's been very generous with them," Po said. "And he and Melanie seem happy.

"Oh, she has, and I think they are," Angela said. "I've just heard him make comments now and then that make me think that he comes up a little short on cash more often than you'd think."

"What about Melanie?" Maggie asked. "I don't know her. Is she involved in the dog scene? What's she do?"

"She likes the dogs, but she doesn't show or anything," Angela said. "She teaches school. Fourth grade, I think."

"Where does she teach?" Po asked.

"I'm not sure now," Angela said. "I thought it was near the house, But I guess I don't know that for sure."

"Kate may know her," Po said to Maggie.

"What about Jarrod?" Po asked.

"He does whatever Mercedes asks him to do for help," Angela said. "She says jump; he asks how high." She laughed. "Although I do think he gets tired of dog duty."

"What makes you say that?" Maggie asked.

"Well, you can just kind of tell. He's very even tempered. But you can kind of see him tightening up after the 50th order from Mercedes. And then he disappears for a while." She smiled again. "I think he does a lot of fishing. And he plays a lot of golf in the summer. And runs a lot of errands in the winter. Whatever it takes to get out of the house."

"But, all in all, he seems supportive of the dogs?"

"I guess so," Angela said.

"Do all the dogs live in the house?" Po asked.

"Not exactly," Angela said. "They built an attached kennel onto the house—a really nice one. It's got tile floors and nice lighting and all. I've never seen better dog quarters."

"And all the dogs stay there?" Po asked.

"At least at night they do," Angela said. "They do sometimes let them run around in the house during the day. But not usually all of them at once."

"But is Fitzgerald typically in the house?" Po asked.

"Yes," Angela said. "He's the exception. He pretty much always stays in the house.

"So that's why Mercedes asked Aaron to put him in the house instead of in the kennel?" Maggie asked.

"I would think so," Angela said. "Plus, she might have been nervous about one of the other dogs getting out. They're not necessarily put to bed for the night in their own runs until later. That way they can roam around a little more and play."

"And they don't fight with each other or anything?" Po asked.

"No, not usually," Angela said. "They're used to being together. Of course, they're careful at feeding time and with treats. Even the best dogs might get aggressive if they're not supervised under those circumstances."

"I hate to ask this, as it may seem personal," Po said. "But does showing dogs pay well? Is it expensive to hire someone to do it?"

Angela laughed. "I don't mind you asking," she said. "It's not like you get rich showing dogs. But the time does cost something. So sometimes owners try to cut corners there and save some money."

"How many hours might you spend?" Po asked.

"Well, like I said, if you're trying to qualify for Westminster, you're on the road every weekend. So that's more expensive. In round numbers, an owner might spend up to $30,000 in a year. A handler who's really working could gross up to $150,000, and might net 20 percent of that."

"How interesting," Po said. "I never realized…"

There was just one more thing she really wanted to know.

"Angela," Po asked, "You haven't said anything about what it was like to work for Mercedes. Did you weigh that at all in your decision to leave."

Angela's face hardened, and Po noticed her hands tightened around the file she was holding.

"Mercedes is not dream to work for," she said shortly. "I think everyone knows that. And yes, I was probably reaching the end of my patience with her. But I tried not to burn any bridges when I left."

"And that wound up being important, given that Mercedes and her family are such important clients for the clinic," Po said.

Angela nodded sharply. "But she still treats me like dirt, just like she does everyone else. You just have to deal with that, I figure."

"Well, thank you for your help, Angela," Maggie said, sensing that Po had reached the end of her questions. "I sure appreciate it."

"Of course," Angela said, but for once she was missing her characteristic smile.

She started to leave, but stopped and looked back when she got to the door. "If there's anything else I can do, just let me know."

When she'd left, Maggie turned to Po. "What do you think?" she asked. "Did we learn anything?"

"I can't decide," Po said thoughtfully.

Maggie smiled. "One of Angela's good points is that she's positive," she said. "She doesn't like to say anything bad about anyone. When she's had a problem with someone, I really have to pull to get it out of her. So, the responses you got to your questions about possible conflicts could be more significant than you'd think."

"Well, we'll see," Po said.

Po was just walking back to her car when her phone rang. "Hi, Kate," she said without preamble. "What did P.J. say?"

"The police are not investigating a disappearance or a kidnapping, Po," Kate said with a serious note in her voice that Po had hardly ever heard. "The homicide team is handling Mercedes' case."

"Homicide?" Po responded, her brain hardly able to consider this possibility. "Homicide?" she said again.

"Yes, Po," Kate said. "And Aaron is heading the list of suspects.

"They found Mercedes' car hidden behind a garage on the west side of town with the keys in it—not more than a three blocks from Aaron's house," Kate said. "Her handbag was inside, nothing taken but the cash."

"They're sure she's dead?" Po asked, struggling to come to terms with this news.

"P.J. said they were as sure as they can be without actually finding the body," Kate said. "But he wouldn't tell me much more. And, of course," she said, "he says to stay out of it, not to worry, and that they are professionals. You know, blah, blah, blah."

Po heard her cover the phone and talk to someone, then she was back. "I have to go, Po. But you might want to call Maggie. I'd bet money they'll be back at the clinic today."

CHAPTER 10

Po dropped her phone back in her bag and considered her next move. Going to tell Maggie the police might be knocking on the door any minute would just make her anxious. Especially when she figured out they were investigating a murder! And Po wasn't sure what Maggie could even do if Po armed her with that information. Until and unless the police showed up, there wasn't much she could do except worry. So, after a few minutes of indecision, she got in her car.

She drove around to the back of the building, and leaving the car running left a note on the ragged front seat of Maggie's beat-up truck. All it said was "call me." She left her number, which Maggie shouldn't need, just in case. "I wouldn't know my own name after the police questioned me about a homicide," she muttered under her breath. "I can't really expect her to remember my number."

And then Po pulled out of the lot.

Ten minutes later, she pulled in the long drive at Eleanor's gracious, well-groomed home. Separated from Canterbury College's campus by a tall wrought-iron fence, the three-story home was built by Elliot Canterbury more than 100 years before. He settled his family there, and built a thriving fur business along the Emerald River. Not content to rest on his business success, the entrepreneur's next move was to found Canterbury College.

The 80-plus year old Queen Bee Eleanor Canterbury lived alone in her family house. But her children and grandchildren—and even great-grandchildren—periodically filled the house. And it didn't get too quiet even between family visits. Eleanor managed to host more than her share of social gatherings, and her elegant home was the perfect place to hold an event. So far, none of the attendees had spotted a ghost or a spirit. But that didn't stop the stories or speculation from students on campus. Every year, at least a couple of students were prepared to swear that they'd seen an unusual light or an unexplained figure floating among the tall oak trees.

Po never entered Eleanor's foyer without thinking about the history and elegance of the structure. But today, she was scarcely distracted by the beauty of the stained glass transom or the one-of-a-kind wooden door that introduced so many other thematic elements in the home. A furniture artisan had done all the woodwork in the home, and had built in many elements, an uncommon approach for the era. She had heard Eleanor give the homes tour once, where she pointed out the characteristic corners and finishes, signature touches that gave the artisan's now collectible pieces their distinctive look.

"I've abandoned Maggie, Eleanor," she said with a wrinkled forehead. "I couldn't figure out how I could help her there. But I feel bad leaving her alone. She may be in for the most stressful day of her life."

"I'm sure you've done the right thing," Eleanor said. "And, if you decide you haven't, we'll load right up and go back. No harm done."

Po nodded and followed Eleanor to the kitchen, where she filled a kettle and set out a selection of teas for Po to pick one.

"Now," she said as they waited for the round red teapot to wail. "Catch me up."

And Po did. Starting with Fitzgerald's disappearance and recapture, and ending with Kate's call.

By the time she finished, they were settled in one of Po's favorite rooms in the house. The conservatory featured panels of tall windows on two walls, flooding the room with light during all daylight hours. The remaining walls were filled with bookshelves, installed by the same craftsman. And a flourishing array of plants gave the space a fresh, green smell that always made Po feel the possibilities of spring, no matter the season.

"So," Po said, with her knack for cutting to the chase. "We need to figure out who really took the dog. That person likely killed Mercedes, too."

Eleanor sipped her tea for a moment and thought. "Do you know where Aaron found Fitzgerald?" she asked.

"I know about where," Po said. "Aaron can probably tell us exactly."

"Well, let's call him up and ask him to show us," Eleanor said. "Maybe there's something out there still that could help us."

She went back to sipping her tea while Po made the call and arranged to pick Aaron up. And then Eleanor picked up her own phone and placed a call.

"Hi, Mike," she said. "How's business?"

"Uh, huh?" "Really?" "Well, I was actually hoping you could do me a favor ..." "That sounds perfect. It will be great to see you. Thank you, Mike." And Eleanor shut her phone.

"Well," she said, straightening her green silk scarf and smiling at Po. "I have a dinner date with the managing editor at the paper tonight. Maybe he'll know something."

The two quilters picked up Aaron 15 minutes later and started the short drive out of town.

"Slow down," he said. "Then take this next right."

The road turned from asphalt to gravel within 20 yards, and Po's bright blue Honda Accord kicked up enough dust that they could smell it even with the vents and windows closed. She thought ruefully that she'd need to be sure to pull through a car wash soon and wished she had more reason to own a car with four-wheel drive. The road petered out before too much longer. Following Aaron's directions, Po pulled over and parked.

"I parked right here," he said. "And I found Fitz just down there a bit."

He climbed out of the car and led the way.

It was a pleasant fall day, sixty-five degrees at least, and the trio stayed plenty warm, especially as Aaron set a fairly brisk pace. Eleanor gripped her carved walking stick as she maneuvered the uneven path. They were near the south edge of Riverfront Park, an area that offered access to five miles of the Emerald River for picnics, hiking, fishing, and other recreation. The Kansas waters boasted 12 types of catfish with the state record for a flathead catfish weighing in at 123 pounds.

"I found him down here, right near the river," he said. "Sometimes people camp down here, and I wonder if he wasn't looking for food. Although," he said a moment later, "he really didn't seem that hungry."

"I don't think Hoover could survive 30 seconds on his own," Po said with a fond smile for her hapless pup. "He depends on getting his kibble delivered twice a day. And he much prefers the sofa cushions to dirt when he's ready for a nap."

"I'd have thought that Fitz would be the same way," Aaron said. "But it didn't seem like he suffered much being out on his own. Angela and I gave him a bath and fed him when I got him back to the clinic." He glanced at them. "I sure didn't want to take him home dirty."

"I can understand that," Po said with an understanding look. She was remembering the confrontation in the reception area, and she was sure Aaron was, too.

"Anyway," he continued, looking slightly reassured, "he really didn't eat that much, considering. So he must have

Dog-Gone Murder

been a better street dog than I expected."

"What made you come here to look?" Eleanor asked.
"This probably sounds dumb," he said. "But I started looking for him in places that I thought I'd like if I were a dog on the run."

Eleanor laughed. "So, what were the key attractions?" she asked.

He shrugged. "I figured it would really help if there were water around. He needed to drink. Plus, people hang out at the river, too, so there might be edible trash or someone around to give him a handout."

"I can see that," Po said. "But that sure leaves a lot of options open."

"I did a lot of looking," he said, a touch defensively.

"You sure did," Po said. "More than anyone. Still, you had to have a bit of luck, I'd say. Your timing had to have been perfect to find him."

Suddenly Aaron looked a little uneasy. "Yeah." And then he got the hard, angry look that Po remembered from their discussion about his visit from the police. She noticed again how much older he looked. And so much tougher. Almost frightening. "Everyone seems to think it was a little too perfect," he said bitterly.

They walked in silence for a few more minutes, and then, "Here's the spot," Aaron said.

To Po, this bend in the river looked very much like the others.

"A lot of folks fish around here," Aaron said. "I wonder if he was eating the leftovers."

"Let's look around," Eleanor suggested. And the three of them split up and searched, "for what, I'm not exactly sure," Po thought, intensely feeling the futility of their hunt.

She kept moving, however, looking for anything that might indicate that someone brought a dog here. "Which is crazy," she thought. "People bring dogs here all the time." And then she heard Aaron yell. "Hey, over here!"

She and Eleanor both hurried over. He was holding the frayed end of a rope. The other end was tied to a slim tree.

"Remember how I told you Fitzgerald had a rope tied around his neck when I found him?" Aaron asked. "I think this could be the other end. Maybe he was tied up here."

"He had a rope around his neck?" Po asked. "I had forgotten that. That makes it pretty clear someone took him, rather than that he just ran away."

"At the time I didn't think at all about it," Aaron said. "I was just happy I found him." He paused, looking at the ground. "I thought that would fix everything."

"We'll get this all figured out," Eleanor said with sympathy.

"Of course we will," Po agreed.

"So," she said. "You took Fitzgerald back to the clinic, right?"

"Uh huh," he said. "Angela made the calls while he was getting dried after the bath. And Mercedes said I should take him to the house."

"Well," Eleanor said jiggling the end of the rope. "Let's take this with us."

CHAPTER 11

Maggie still hadn't called when they dropped Aaron off at his apartment. Po decided it would be better not to invade the clinic asking questions about rope if the police had in fact shown up there. So she dropped Eleanor off and headed home.

The key, she thought, is to stay busy. Waiting for the phone to ring never makes the time pass. So she put together the ingredients for soup in her slow cooker, dumped flour, water, yeast and salt in her bread maker, and left the kitchen appliances working so she could go work herself in her studio. Looking at her first efforts at the leaves she'd added to her tree quilt, she decided she wasn't happy. Too regular. Too predictable. Too ... and she tried again.

This time she moved straight to playing with the fabrics she'd picked, which often led to happy accidents and original designs. Anytime her thoughts strayed to Maggie, she drew them sharply back to the moment and the challenge at hand, refocusing on her second-generation pile of leaves. Which despite her distraction was growing on her. So much, in fact, that she started laying out a few along the next branch of her tree. Eventually, the progress on the project held her complete attention, as it almost always could. So she jumped a little when the phone rang.

"Hi Po," said Kate. Po heard the worry in Kate's voice. "Did you talk to Maggie?"

"I actually didn't," Po admitted. "I couldn't figure out how I could make it any better. So I just left a note, asking her to call me as soon as she could."

"I'm sure you were right, Po," Kate said. "I sort of had that thought. That's why I keep calling you instead of her. I imagine what she might be doing right at that moment, and decide it's not the time to interrupt." There was a short moment of silence. "But it's killing me!" Kate blurted. "I can't believe they're investigating Maggie and her clinic. Those are the most caring people in the world!"

Po smiled, despite herself. Kate's passion for justice and deep caring for her friends got her into trouble sometimes, but it also made her Kate.

"So, what have you learned?" Po asked. "Was it P.J. who gave you the scoop?"

P.J. Flannigan had been Kate's on-again off-again flame all through high school. And when she'd come back to town, he not so surprisingly reappeared on the scene—just as tall, dark and handsome as ever, and with the same cheeky smile. Although now he was an officer in the local Police Department, with a more subtle understanding of human nature and a lot more experience and responsibility than he'd had at 17. Po thought he was all the better for it. But she tried to keep those thoughts mostly to herself. Or, at the very least, limited to the conversations she had late at night with Kate's mom, when she gave her best friend updates on her now grown little girl–and reassured her that she was still looking out for her.

"Uh huh," Kate confirmed. "He came over when he got off last night, and he said that the department was pursuing the investigation with diligence. You know how he gives me that 'I can neither confirm nor deny' stuff. But then he got a call during our run this morning, and had to go in early. I could tell from his end of the conversation what was happening. So I called you on my way to work."

"I'm sure he'd never guess that you'd do that," Po said wryly.

"You know and I know that he knows that's exactly what I did," Kate said. "And I'd do it again this minute."

"Well, thank you for learning what you could from that sweet young man of yours," Po said. "But don't get in trouble. I like him."

"I like him, too, Po," Kate said. "So much that I think I'll see what he's doing tonight. Maybe I can learn some more from him. Plus, I'm in the mood for Italian."

Dog-Gone Murder

Po attempted to listen while Kate rattled on about her plans for the rest of the day. It was at least 30 seconds before Kate realized Po wasn't hearing her.

"What is it?" Kate asked.

"What?" Po asked, snapping out of her reverie.

"I can tell you haven't heard a thing I've said," Kate laughed. "What are you thinking about?"

"It's probably nothing," Po said with a shrug. "But I can't stop thinking about Aaron saying no one was home when he took Fitzgerald back. I wonder where they all were."

"Excellent question," Kate said. "I'll look into it."
Po frowned. "You know how P.J. feels about you interfering in an investigation," she said. "And you know, I'm not that wild about the idea, either."

"Come on, Po," never-to-be-tamed Kate said with a smile. "Don't worry."

And she was gone.

Po smiled, set down the phone on the edge of the table, and shook her head at her impulsive goddaughter. And then she went back to the designs she'd laid out. Before more than half an hour passed, her phone rang again, and during this call she had very few reasons to smile.

"Maggie," she said. "Are you OK?"

"Oh, Po."

"I've got soup on. Come over. Maybe I can help," Po said. And with very little more persuading, a very upset Maggie agreed.

Po opened the heavy front door and made sure the porch

light was on. The fall nights were starting to darken earlier. Then she went and started mixing her special occasion drink: a vodka martini. She floated an apple slice on top and had it ready to hand to Maggie when she walked in, looking tired and strained.

Maggie collapsed moments later into one of Po's comfortable club chairs. Po carried over a plate of Havarti cheese and water crackers and joined her. Then she waited patiently for Maggie to open the conversation.

"So," she said finally. "I got your note, of course."

Po just nodded.

"And you knew," Maggie said. "How'd you know?"

"Kate called just after I walked out," Po said. "I thought it would just worry you more."

Maggie sighed. "You were probably right," she said after a pause. "But, man."

Silence ensued for a while. But finally Po couldn't take it any more. "So, what all happened?"

"Well, for starters, they shut me down for the day," Maggie said. "Angela spent the first two hours doing nothing but calling to reschedule with everyone, or taking calls and arranging for our clients to go to Dr. Conrad's practice for immediate care." She sighed again. "Just what I need with my current cash flow problem."

She took a piece of cheese and a sip of her drink. "Then, one officer started interviewing each staff member in one of the exam rooms, while another started taking pictures of every room. They took every angle. They dusted every surface for fingerprints." Another silence. "It's going to take hours to get it cleaned up again."

"Did they say what they were looking for?" Po asked.

"They just kept saying they were investigating a homicide," Maggie said. "They think someone killed Mercedes, Po. Not that she decided she had enough and left for the Caribbean without warning. Not that she got sudden amnesia and can't find her way home. They think she's dead!"

"I was shocked, too," Po said.

"And apparently they think there's some chance she died at my clinic! Can you imagine?! It's impossible…. I tried to tell Officer Rainey that. It was like talking to a brick."

She paused to take a bite of the cheese she'd been waving as she talked.

"They asked me how long everyone had worked at my clinic. Whether any of them had a police record. Whether anyone had a particular problem with Mercedes. There were a million questions."

"Did they take pictures of anything specific, or just the whole place?" Po asked.

"Well," Maggie paused to think. "I was a little distracted. But I did notice that they were taking a close look at the doors. I think they took pictures of the handles and latches and keypad."

She thought again. "They seemed interested in the drug safe, too." A momentary pause. "But Po, you've got to understand, they seemed interested in every square inch. They even took pictures of the storage closet."

"Maybe they really didn't know what they were looking for," Po said. "So they were looking at everything. That could mean that they don't really have any evidence that your clinic is involved, for sure."

"They apparently had enough evidence to convince a judge," Maggie said. "They had a warrant. So I had no choice about letting them search. And they closed the clinic for the day."

"So, they had a reasonable suspicion they might find something there," Po said. "They've learned something that makes them think she was at the clinic before she disappeared. But that doesn't mean they're right."

Maggie lapsed back into silence.

"Are you OK, Maggie?" Po asked finally. "I can't imagine how upset you must be feeling."

"I'm exhausted, Po," she said. "I just can't deal with all this."

She shook her head. "Poor Aaron. They asked me a lot about him. I think he's their top suspect. And I know he wouldn't hurt a fly. So that's a huge problem."

Po thought about the flashes of anger she'd seen, and speculated privately that if the police had seen similar demonstrations, they'd think differently about Aaron's propensity for violence. At those moments he looked less like the quiet young man they knew who was always ready to help out and more like a towering figure with the strength to do damage. Unaware of Po's momentary preoccupation, Maggie continued.

"Then there's the business I lost today," she said. "And the bad publicity. And the consultant I hired is coming tomorrow. The financial picture is looking worse than ever."

"And then," she continued "we're going to have to do clean up before anything else. The clinic is a total mess."

"Well, that part I can help with," Po said. "I'll come first thing. And maybe we're learning more that can help at this very minute. Phoebe is at the Women's Club meeting at the country club tonight, sniffing out information about who else could be angry enough at Mercedes to do her bodily harm. And Eleanor is having dinner with Mike Walters, the managing editor at the paper. So maybe she'll know more by tomorrow, too."

Tears filled Maggie's eyes. "You guys are so wonderful," she said. "What would I ever do without you?"

Po smiled. "We sure find our way together, don't we?" she said. "But that's what friends are for. Now how about some soup?"

Maggie wiped her eyes and gave Po a small smile. "I'd love some," she said. "But I'm worried about getting home as it is. I am so exhausted. I might fall down. I think I'd better just go home and go to bed. I need to get up early to get the place cleaned up again."

"I thought you had blocked out a bunch of your schedule tomorrow, to see the consultant," Po said.

"I did," Maggie said.

"Well, then, why don't I meet you there 30 minutes before you open. We can do a quick pass through the reception area, so if someone shows up unexpectedly, it'll look OK. Then your team can help clean up the rest while you're busy."

Maggie thought it over. "You're right, Po. I don't have to have the whole place clean at 8. And I don't have to do it all myself." She smiled again. "Boy, I need you to help me think it through tonight."

"Tomorrow you'll feel better," Po said. "We can regroup and decide what to do next."

She packaged up a container of the soup and a chunk of bread in a paper bag and handed it to Maggie, giving her a hug on the way out.

"It's going to be OK," she said.

"I sure hope you're right," Maggie said. And as Maggie walked out to her truck, Po could see the stress in every line of her body.

"Me, too, Maggie," she said quietly as she watched her friend of 20 years walk out. "I sure hope I'm right."

CHAPTER 12

Po was sitting in the same spot she'd occupied during the conversation with Maggie when Max knocked softly on the front door and let himself in. She was happy to see him tonight. He came into the room, following her call of greeting, and squeezed her shoulders.

"Tough day?" he asked, looking at her still-furrowed brow.

"You could say that," she said with a small laugh. "You are just the person to put my mind back at ease, though."

Under her direction from the sofa, Max ladled the soup into two bowls, put together a quick salad and sliced the bread Po had baked. Within minutes the two of them were ensconced

Dog-Gone Murder

at one end of the table, eating the hearty soup. Po gave a deep sigh as she felt her body start to relax, degree by degree.

Max put down his spoon for a moment, taking her hand and giving it a little squeeze. "Now," he said, with his characteristic smile, "what's going on?"

She had talked to Max just before she'd dropped into bed the night before, and had tried to fill him in about Mercedes' disappearance and the conversation with Aaron. So now Po recapped her visit to Maggie's clinic and the discovery of Mercedes' car while they ate.

Spurred to greater levels of detail by thoughtful questions from Max, she explained her trip to Eleanor's house and their investigation of the site where Aaron found Fitzgerald. They finished up their dinner, cleared the dirty plates, leaving them on the counter, and moved back to the sofa to finish their conversation. Po found Max's closeness comforting and she recounted some bits of her conversations with Maggie that she'd overlooked. And finally, Po told Max she was planning to go help Maggie clean the clinic the next morning.

"You're a wonderful friend," he said with a smile.

"The way you say that makes it sound like a bad thing," Po said. "Is there a rebuke in the offing?"

"Of course not," Max said. "I love that you're so caring. That's one of the incredibly attractive things about you." He paused, looking worried. "But this is no light matter," he said. "A woman has been killed. And you're in the thick of it again, it looks to me."

Po had to acknowledge that she'd been involved in more violent episodes than the demographics of the area should allow. Crestwood was such a pleasant, safe town. And yet there was the time she found Owen Hill's dead body outside of Selma's quilt store during her morning run. It was during that investigation that she'd really gotten to know Max.

And then about a year later she and the Queen Bees helped defend Picasso, the owner of The French Quarter, when he was wrongly accused of murdering his wife. And then the time they'd made all the quilts for Adele's bed and breakfast after her brother died and discovered the murderer along the way. She did seem to find herself faced with deadly weapons more often than she'd like. But still....

"I'm just helping Maggie," Po said. "If I had any helpful information, I would go right to the police. I don't know a thing. I wish I did."

"It's that wishing that's bothering me," Max said.

Po knew he had her best interests at heart. But she could not—would not—stand by and do nothing if she could help a dear friend in trouble. And she knew Max understood her well enough to know that was true.

"Do you know who benefits from Mercedes' death, if she's dead?" Po asked finally.

Max looked troubled. "I've been hoping you wouldn't think to ask me that," he said. "But other people are asking, too."

"Really?" Po said. "Who?"

"The detective in charge of Mercedes' case," he said, with the furrow in his brow getting even deeper. Then he looked at her, and his expression grew warm again.

"I've got to get a few things cleared up," he said. "And then we can talk about it."

And Po agreed to that, knowing it was the best she could do for the time being.

"I suppose it's no good asking you to start locking your doors," he said on his way out. He'd made this sensible suggestion more than once or twice before. Po had stubbornly refused. There was something about making the change that seemed to admit fear. Or worse, that her world had dramatically changed and that she had to release her long-held faith in the goodness and kindness of the people who formed her community. And even today, with the knowledge that Mercedes was likely dead, she would not yield.

"No," she said. "No, it's no good."

CHAPTER 13

Po slept fretfully and was up early, so she hit the streets. A fog hung over the fall morning, and a damp, slightly musty smell seemed to fill the dips in her path and her hard-working lungs as she ran through the quiet. Her mind slowed, as it almost always did, falling into the rhythm of her steps and relaxing into her routine.

As she turned back toward home, her thoughts turned back toward her plans for the day, starting with another trip to Maggie's clinic to talk with Angela. She'd been thinking about the list Angela had given her of people who had access to the clinic during the time that Fitzgerald had escaped or been stolen. "I have to admit, I'm leaning toward stolen," Po muttered to herself, and she cooled down, walking up her own block and back to her front steps.

Thirty minutes later, she headed back out, dressed in her favorite jeans and a million layers in shades of gray, so she could adjust for the temperature fluctuation they predicted as the day went on. She loaded two buckets and a box of cleaning materials into the car and started off, but she got only halfway out of the driveway before she pulled back in and ran into the house, emerging two minutes later with the digital camera her daughter and son-in-law had bought her for Christmas.

Maggie's truck was at the clinic when she arrived. "No surprise there," she thought to herself.

"Good morning," she said as she walked in the door and saw Maggie filling a bucket using a faucet in the cleaning closet off the reception area.

"Morning," Maggie returned.

"Did you get any rest?" Po asked.

"I slept for a while," Maggie said. "but I woke up early. So I figured I might as well get on this."

"Before you start," Po said, "I'd like to take pictures. If the police think there's something to look at, I'd like to see it, too."

Maggie arched an eyebrow. "Really? I keep telling them there's nothing to see."

"I know," Po said. "But still. It seems safer. Armed with data, rather than not. I'll be quick so we can get going."

She pulled out a thermos of hot, strong coffee. "Here, pour this while I take these."

Maggie smiled. "You know just how to sweeten me up, don't you."

"You know what we forgot?" Maggie called over her shoulder a few minutes later.

Po had started taking pictures of the reception area. She tried to get an overview of the room from each angle. And now she was taking a series of close ups of the inside and outside of the door. "No," she said. "What?"

"We didn't go to Selma's last night," Maggie said.

"Oh, man," Po said. "I didn't think of it once."

The Queen Bees often gathered on Tuesday nights at Selma's informally, just to sew in the company of their friends. And while it was unusual for the whole group to make it, Po hardly ever missed. "We must have had quite a day to throw me off that much," she said with a laugh.

"You're telling me," Maggie said, drinking her coffee still.

Po had moved onto the reception desk, snapping shots of everything she could see. "No appointment book these days," she thought.

"Maggie," she said. "Could you print me a list of all the people who've been in with their pets in the last month?"

Maggie sighed. "All right," she said without enthusiasm. "I've been printing endless reports for the accountant. I might as well print one more for you." She walked to her office.

Po had pictures of everything she could even think of taking in the reception area. And nothing seemed out of place to her. "Maybe this is a waste of time," she muttered to herself as she flipped through them in view mode, making sure there was something stored there. Suddenly she came across some pictures of her daughter and granddaughter, and she smiled. The Fourth of July holiday when her kids and their families had come to visit seemed like such a long time away. She had a sudden longing for the warm, languid days of summer, when none of this trouble had disrupted her friends' lives.

Just then, Maggie walked back out of her office, holding a sheaf of papers. "Here you go," she said. "The last month of appointments. I just made another printout of a report I had done already. So it shows how much they spent at each visit also."

"Thank you," Po said. "And perfect timing. We can clean up out here now. Then I'll take pictures of the rest. Just in case."

Po tucked the printouts into the tote she'd brought in loaded with rags and paper towels and glass cleaner. Then she refocused on the job of the moment, shining up the front door, cleaning the glass and wiping the dusting powder off the doorknobs, inside and out. Maggie was still mopping the ceramic tile when she finished, so Po started wiping down the front desk and then the waterproof pads on the benches and small end tables in the reception area. Finally, she wiped down the top of the curved wall that separated the dog area from the cat side.

When she finished, Po moved on to take pictures in Maggie's office, every exam room, and then in the treatment area, the surgical suite and the boarding area. She shot close-ups of the inside and outside of the staff entrance and the back door. And of anything else that looked as though it received attention during the homicide team's search the day before. There seemed to be more fingerprint dust than expected in the pharmacy. She made a mental note to ask Maggie about that later.

When she finished, she worked her way back to the front of the clinic and found that Angela had arrived.

"I didn't expect to see you here, Po," she said. "And you're both here early."

"Angela is the first team member I've ever had who almost always beats me in," Maggie said with a smile.

"I'm an early riser," Angela shrugged. "And if I get in here and get things organized, we can keep our days running smoothly."

"Always a good thing," Po agreed.

"So, we've cleaned up this front room," Maggie said. "If you guys could help with my office, we should be fine when Maya arrives at nine. She's the consultant who's coming to talk with me," she said as an aside to Angela. "Then I don't think we have any appointments scheduled for me, right?"

"Right," Angela said. "We do need to get the exam rooms cleaned up fairly soon, though. At 10 we've got a pre-adoption meeting set up with Mrs. Lynn. She's thinking of getting a dog and wants to make sure her cats can deal with it OK. Catie is going to meet with her. And then we've got three weigh-ins this afternoon, I think." She turned to Po to explain. "We're testing a new weight-loss program with a few of our really obese patients. I just know they're going to feel so much better if they slim down a little. But it's hard for pet owners. So often, we express our love by giving treats or snacks. And it's hard to fit in long enough walks to counteract that."

Po looked from Angela to Maggie. "I know it probably won't

do any good, but I still wanted to talk with everybody here about that code list you gave me, Angela. Can I use one of the exam rooms to do that?"

"Sure," Angela said. "Maggie said you wanted to do that today. Just let me know when you're ready. I can introduce you to anyone you don't know."

She turned to Maggie. "Do you want to do morning rounds today?"

Every morning the small team at the clinic met to talk about how any hospitalized patients were doing, what care they needed, and which clients and patients they expected to see during the day. This 15 minute stand-up meeting set the stage for a smooth running day, and helped their team make sure none of the care their patients counted on them for fell through the cracks.

"I think we'd better," Maggie said. "After the disruption yesterday everyone will be feeling jumpy. And we still won't have things back to normal today. I think we'd better take the time to talk about that, and about our patients. That's what we're here for, after all."

"OK," Angela said. "I'll let everyone know. We'll be ready to get together at the normal time." She turned back to Po. "Actually," she said. "If you just came to the meeting, everyone could meet you then. That might be more efficient. And it's only about 15 minutes away."

Po had just heard a car door slam, and then she heard another. She realized the practice team was gathering for the day. "That sounds great," she said. "Thank you."

At 8 o'clock sharp the morning team was gathered in the

treatment area, leaning up against counters and treatment tables, chatting. Although she couldn't hear anything of what they were saying, Po felt a certain tension when she walked into the room—despite the quiet chorus of good mornings for Dr. Maggie and Angela. She felt certain they were discussing the search the day before.

When Maggie started to talk, the room grew quiet.

She quickly ran through the status of the hospitalized pets. There were only a couple. Wednesday mornings were usually reserved for surgeries, but they'd not scheduled any for today, because of the consultant's initial visit. And they'd redirected clients with emergencies the day before, because of the police investigation. So, all in all, they had fewer cases to discuss than normal.

They did, of course, have plenty of other issues to discuss. So Maggie opened by talking about the events of the day before.

"You were all here yesterday," she said. "So you know the police investigated the practice with the thought that someone here could somehow be part of Mrs. Richardson's disappearance," Maggie said. "I have, of course, reassured them that this can't be the case. Still, I appreciate all of your help and cooperation yesterday. Now, today, I'd like to try to get back to normal, as much as possible. Unfortunately, there will not be a lot of glamour involved." She won a mild chuckle from the group. "We need to clean up, obviously."

Angela spoke up. "It won't take too long," she said. "And we were talking about doing some fall cleaning anyway. This will give us the perfect opportunity."

"We've also got guests today," Maggie went on. "Many of you know Portia Paltrow. She's a long time client. Normally you see her with Hoover. And she's my dear friend. She's trying to help us figure out what's going on here and how to stay out of trouble."

Po nodded a little, and smiled generally at the crowd. And she could see some friendly smiles in return, including from Catie, the young woman who'd given her the tour of the back of the hospital the last time she'd visited.

"Po will be talking with each of you today, to learn more about our schedules and security and about how we work."

Maggie went on. "This is also the day that I'll be meeting with the consultant, you'll remember. That's why we have so few visits scheduled. She'll be helping me think about how we can work more efficiently."

Po thought the response to this seemed a bit less enthusiastic, and resolved to ask about that, too, as long as she was at it.

Angela stepped in again. "We do have some technician appointments scheduled," she said. "Mrs. Lynn is coming for pre-adoption counseling. Tess, I wrote you in to lead that appointment. We also have three weigh-ins, Catie. You'd done so much with that program, it seems like you're perfect to do those today.

"So," Maggie said. "Thank you all for your poise yesterday. By tomorrow, I hope our schedule will be back to normal."

And with that they adjourned. Although Po, who lingered slightly behind Angela and Maggie, who were still strategizing about the best use of the team's time for the day, noticed that a few quiet conversations ensued as soon as it appeared that there was no one to monitor the discussion.

Po arrived back in the reception area just in time to meet Maya, Maggie's consultant, and exchange pleasantries about the weather. Then Maya and Maggie headed for Maggie's office.

"So, Po," Angela said. "Do you want to talk with people in any particular order?"

"I don't really have a clear plan," Po said. "Is there an approach that would be less disruptive? I don't want to be any more bother than absolutely necessary."

Angela's cell phone started to vibrate, and she checked it surreptitiously to see the caller ID and then chose not to answer. But within just a minute it began to buzz again. "I'm sorry," she said. "but can you excuse me for just a minute? I've really got to take this."

Po nodded, and wandered off to sit in a corner of the reception area and think about what questions she needed to ask to get a clearer picture of what was—or was not—going on at the clinic. She vaguely heard Angela talking quietly as she worked her way to the back of the hospital.

Five minutes later, she had her list ready. Angela wasn't back. "She must have gotten sidetracked," she thought. And she decided to just go find someone to talk to on her own, rather than waiting for Angela to facilitate. "And I may run into her around the first bend anyway," she thought.

Po started for the back of the hospital, but paused next to the side door as she passed it, thinking again about who could have entered that way without causing any damage. And as

Dog-Gone Murder

she stood there, she suddenly heard Angela's voice right outside.

"Who do you think you are?" she said. "I don't have to take this from you!"

And then her strident tone suddenly changed.

"I know, I know. I get it. Just calm down. I don't want any more trouble."

She sounded like she was just on the other side of the door, and Po was certain she had no idea she could be overheard. She certainly didn't want Angela to find her lurking there. So, heart thumping, Po moved away from the door as quickly as she could, trying to duck around the next corner as casually as possible. And she was just in time, because she heard the door open.

Po was still close enough to hear Angela's phone snap shut, and then to hear her take two shaky breaths. She decided the best course was to turn around and act as though she'd just started down the hall.

"Oh," she said, feigning surprise when she saw Angela. "I was just coming to tell you that I'm ready."

"Great," Angela said. Po thought she looked upset, but it was hard to tell for sure. "Let me show you which room you can use, and then I'll bring Catie to talk with you."

"OK," Po said. But while she waited, she wondered: Who could that have been on the phone? What kind of trouble?

Po thought for the hundredth time how lucky Maggie had been to find such a warm—and still efficient—team member to head up her office team and keep her days organized. And Po had known Maggie long enough to see what a difference a strong team leader could make.

It had to be a relief, she thought, not to be in charge of every detail anymore. To have someone else doing scheduling and tracking inventory and taking care of some of those details of keeping a business running. And a complicated business at that. And it seemed as if Angela found the work very satisfying. She really treated the clinic as if it were her own. "I'm overreacting," she thought. "What kind of problem could Angela possibly have?"

Within one minute, Angela came back with Catie in tow, effectively cutting Po's reverie short. "Hi, Mrs. Paltrow," she said.

Po remembered how friendly Catie was from her quick tour during her last visit to the clinic. "Hi, Catie," she said. "Thanks for coming to talk with me." She hesitated, not sure where to begin. Then she dug Angela's list of code owners out of her bag and handed it to Catie.

"I'm trying to make sure we've got a complete list of everyone who might have access to the clinic," she said. "Do you know of anyone else who would know how to get in?"

Catie glanced at the sheet, and shook her head. "No," she said. "It looks like everyone is on the list."

"Is there anyone you think who could guess your code?" Po asked. "Or do you know anyone else's? Or does anyone else in the clinic know yours?"

Catie looked sharply at her. "I'm not trying to get anybody in trouble," Po said quickly, trying to clarify. "I'm just trying to think about all the ways someone might be able to get in without being on this list."

The young woman looked somewhat mollified, and she pushed her sleek blond hair back over her shoulder. "You key in your code anytime you're the one who locks up," she said. "Someone might be able to watch and figure it out. But what would be the point? They have their own code."

Po nodded. "Is your code the same for all the doors?" she asked.

"Uh huh," Catie confirmed. "There's a different code for the drug safe," she said. "And they change that one and our codes for the door anytime an employee leaves the clinic," she said.

"Do you have drugs here that someone might want?" Po asked, feeling a little surprised.

"Well, we have ketamine," Catie said. "That's what people would be most interested in, at least."

"Oh," Po said, feeling a bit out of her league. "Why?"

"It's a hallucinogenic," Catie said. "But the trip doesn't last long. About an hour. Still, it's a popular club drug."

"I see," Po said. "I didn't realize..."

"Yeah, a lot of people don't," Catie said. "But I know Dr. Maggie and Angela keep a close eye on our drug log, and I bet that's one reason why. And," she went on, "they require drug testing for new hires, and stuff like that."

Feeling a little overwhelmed with the new information—and the enormity of the things she didn't even know to ask about—Po wrapped up her first interview there, and resolved to come back to this topic with Maggie later. It seems she had quite a lot to learn about the drugs available in a veterinary hospital. Her phone interrupted that thought.

"Hi, Po. It's me," said Kate. "Are you busy?"

"Hi, Kate," she said. "Never too busy for you. What do you need?"

"I've got an update," she said. "About where they found Mercedes' car. The police found it near Ninth and Walnut."

"I know where that is," Po said. "But surely it wasn't just parked on the street."

"No," Kate said. "It was behind a garage. The owners finally called the police to complain that the car was blocking them in."

"How did you find out?" Po asked.

"P.J. let it slip," Kate said. "He had to run out in a hurry, and I managed to sneak in a few questions on his way out the door."

"He won't be mad with you, will he?" Po asked, always concerned for her goddaughter's happiness—and wishing for a wedding, if the truth must be told.

"Not if you don't go apologizing about my nosiness the next time you see him," Kate said.

"Did he say anything else?" Po asked.

"Besides Mercedes' handbag, he said they found Fitzgerald's leash and harness," Kate said.

"I don't know quite what to make of it," Po said.

"Me neither," agreed Kate. "But I'll ask him about it again tonight and call you in the morning," Kate said. "I'm still trying to learn where Jarrod and Jack Francis were," she said. "Nothing but dead ends so far."

"Oh," Po said with surprise. "I hadn't thought of this until now, but I actually saw Jarrod on the day Mercedes disappeared."

She explained about his visit to the hardware store and the bait for the fishing trip. "Angela mentioned that he likes to fish," she said.

"Great, that gives me somewhere to go next," Kate said, and she went back to class.

Po took a minute to write down some notes on the back of the printouts Maggie had given her about what Kate had said, and about what she'd learned from Catie. She was beginning to feel as if her brain were like a full bucket. Any additional information might just pour over the sides. With the key points committed to paper, she asked Angela to track down the next team member. She talked to each of the next three in turn: technician Julie Stepford, veterinary assistant Tess Johnston, receptionist Lynne Wilson. Aaron didn't work on Wednesdays, so he wasn't there. Which just left Angela.

"So," Angela said as she walked into the room. "Did you learn anything that will help?"

"I don't think so," Po said, with a little shake of her head. "It's so hard to know what to ask."

"Almost anyone might have shared their code with a friend or boyfriend or something," Angela said. "But these are all good people. They're very devoted to caring for people's pets, and they don't want to hurt Dr. Maggie."

"I know you're right," Po sighed. "But still, if we can find anything that will help. Poor Maggie is so upset."

She paused a moment. "Angela, I know this is silly, but I didn't realize you guys had any drugs here that would be attractive for theft or resale. And the police sure seemed to be all over that drug safe. Is that why?"

"Probably," Angela said. "That's one reason Dr. Maggie requires drug testing when she hires. Of course we have a drug log, where we track our use of controlled substances. So that's another precaution against someone on the team dipping into the stores. We try to be careful about security, too," she went on. "We have a security system. We installed good outdoor lighting. We made sure the entryway provided as much visibility from the street as possible. Stuff like that."

"That makes sense," Po said.

"How's it going with the consultant?" Po asked. "Can you tell?"

"Dr. Maggie hasn't emerged at all yet," Angela said. "I hope it's going OK."

"Is there anything to worry about?" Po asked.

"I hope not," Angela said. "This is a good group of people. And we can't really work too much harder. So that consultant better not be preaching too much belt tightening."

"Oh, surely when Maggie said she'd look at efficiency, she wouldn't mean cutting back people or hours," Po said, with sudden understanding.

"Well, I hope you're right," Angela said. "I don't think Dr. Maggie would do that. But I don't know the consultant. She might not realize how hard everyone around here is working already."

Po smiled at her. "You do a great job," she said. "All of you. And I know Maggie knows that. She says so all the time."

Angela gave her a tight smile. "I guess you're right," she said. "I'll try to stop worrying."

Dog-Gone Murder

"Well, it's not like there hasn't been plenty to worry about lately, right?" Po said with a little laugh. " I appreciate your help today."

"Well, the sooner we can get back to normal the better," Angela said, with a more natural smile. "It's our mission to help people. And we can't do that if we're tied up in a police investigation."

"No one does that better than you do," Po said, squeezing her shoulder. "It's unusual for Angela to prickle," she thought. "Still," she shrugged, "who wouldn't with the week they've had?"

Maggie was still sequestered with the consultant when Po left, and Po debated what to do. She was dying to leave another "call me" note in Maggie's truck. She'd just leave the message on Maggie's cell phone, except she wasn't sure Maggie had remembered to turn it off. "The last thing I want to do is interrupt that meeting," Po thought. In the end, she decided she'd just have to hope Maggie would call to give her an update when she got free.

Po tried not to get in the habit of going to Marla's all the time. When she walked through the door, it was too hard to resist all the delicious offerings. Fresh-from-the-oven scones and croissants and apricot Danish. She wasn't opposed to a nice fruit tart with her coffee. Or, if it were late morning, a slice of quiche or her all-time favorite, eggs Benedict.

Max teased her that her idea of variety in breakfast was to substitute smoked salmon for smoked ham. And he wasn't all wrong. She could easily make that rich meal a daily ritual.

And that would be a bad trade in the long-term health world from her typical fruit or oatmeal. So she tried not to go except with Leah on Sundays. Today, however, she deserved a treat. Needed one, in fact. Badly.

So after she left the clinic, she parked down by Daisy's flower shop, the closest spot she could find to the bakery. "I know it was a tough conversation," she thought as she eyed the planters outside, "but boy, the mums sure look so much nicer." In the early days, Daisy would leave dilapidated plastic daisies in her outdoor planters for months at a time. The Elderberry Shop Owners' Corporation finally appointed Owen Hill to talk to her about maintaining a little higher standard for her displays. That was just days before Po herself found Owen's dead body in the alley behind Selma's fabric store. She shook off the thought.

Two minutes later, Po found herself at Marla's bakery and went in for some coffee and to peruse the pastry counter. "Breakfast is always a good option for lunch," she thought to herself.

"Hi, Po," welcomed Marla from behind the counter.

"Hi, Marla," returned Po. "Beautiful weather we're having, don't you think?"

"This warm fall weather is great for business," Marla agreed. "It's so nice to be out in it. People are happy to walk around down here."

"Well, who can blame them?" Po said with a smile.

"I wish I weren't so short-handed," Marla said with a frown. "One of my girls called in sick. I bet she was out partying too late. Disgraceful, the lack of responsibility in this next generation. Into the party scene. Loyalty to a boss always comes second to their personal agendas, I say."

Marla leaned a little closer as she rang up Po's coffee and the sinful cream cheese Danish that she hadn't been able to resist at the last moment. "Here it comes," Po thought.

"I heard that young boy working for Maggie found the missing dog," she said knowingly.

"Yes, that's true," Po confirmed. "Aaron was so wonderful. He simply would not quit looking until he found Fitzgerald."

"It was just a couple days before that Mercedes gave him a big dressing down for letting the dog get hurt, though," Marla rejoined. "At least that's the way I heard it. And now she's gone missing…. That'll be $6.32."

"Hmm," Po said, trying not to commit herself to anything concrete as she handed over her debit card.

"Well, that's all interesting, isn't it," Marla said. "You've got to wonder."

"Wonder what?" Po asked, in spite of herself.

"Wonder what he had to gain by stealing the dog, of course," Marla said, looking at her surprised.

"Aaron couldn't have done that," Po said. "He's so kind, and has been such a help to Maggie."

"You're such a wonderful person, Po," Marla said, handing her the coffee and pastry and clearly dismissing her. "You never think anything bad about anyone. But I have an inside source on this one."

"Really?" Po said. "Who is that?"

"Why, Mrs. Abernathe was at the clinic that day, when Mercedes told that young man never to come near her dog again. And she saw the look on his face. She said, sure as the day she was born, he decided right that minute to get revenge on her for embarrassing him that way."

Po was too shocked to even respond, and Marla went right on.

"Maybe Mercedes figured it out about the dog, and that's why he kidnapped her."

"Aaron?"

"Why, of course. That's what everyone is saying."

"But…" Po tried to get her footing in the conversation, but not in time. Marla had moved on to her next customer with her conviction of Aaron firmly in place in her mind.

"Shoot," Po thought. "And I bet she's right. I'm sure that's what a lot of people are thinking."

Po took a deep breath and settled into her booth, vowing to drink what was left of her coffee and enjoy it. "Good thing I got the grande," she muttered to herself. "There will be time to muddle and stew after." And she was as good as her word, enjoying the Zen-like focus on each swallow of the rich, full flavor and the robust steam that wafted up from the bowl-sized mug as she sipped.

The comings and goings of people in and out of the bakery didn't rouse her. At least, not until she happened to notice Jarrod Richardson at the front of the line, buying the same large latte she'd chosen, but to go, and two muffins. It was the discussion of the muffins that flagged her subconscious about his presence.

As he left the bakery and walked back through her field of vision past the large front window, Po noticed his tall carriage and brisk stride. And he had a gentle-seeming smile, just as she had when he passed the window of Selma's. Po did a quick calculation. Less than a week ago. "But, my," she thought. "What a terrible week. And worse for him than us."

Po chewed on this thought. Then, acting on impulse, she maneuvered into her jacket, grabbed the handles of her handbag and scooted across the bench to the aisle, slugging down one last greedy glug of coffee and looking somewhat regretfully at the last third. "Oh, well," she sighed. And she headed out onto the street.

"This is crazy," she thought. "It's Kate who's out following people and getting into trouble. Not me." But there she was. Jarrod was moving quickly. He'd taken a couple of quick drinks of the hot coffee before he left Marla's and was making good time, now that there was no danger of it splashing down his hand as he went.

Po followed him down the road, trying to seem casual. She was surprised when he strode past the hardware store. "Hmm," she thought. "That's where I assumed he was headed. And he's beginning to run out of options."

And then with a quick look around, he ducked through the door of the stationery shop. "Well, I don't really want to go in there with him," thought Po. So she slid into Selma's instead, waved a cheery hello to Susan, who was busy cutting swaths from three bolts of fabric for a customer, and busied herself pretending to look at the bolts of chintz near the window, while she really watched the sidewalk for Jarrod to emerge. She hadn't been at her post for long, when suddenly a furious looking Jack Francis materialized on the sidewalk right in front of her, scowling. He pushed his way through the door of Elderberry Road's upscale stationery store, The Ink Spot, and disappeared from her view. She watched just a moment longer and then followed her impulse for the second time in less than 20 minutes. "I really am getting to be as bad as Kate," she thought as she left the fabric store and headed into the stationery shop after him.

As she walked in, she saw Helen, the storeowner, behind the counter. Then her eyes fixed, as Helen's were, on the two men standing in the center of the small shop, both red-faced, hands clenched.

"You did it, didn't you?" Jack Francis was shouting at Jarrod as the door swung shut behind Po. Po felt the eyes of the stray shopper in one corner flicker her way, but only for a second. And the circling men didn't even notice that she'd joined them.

"You did it. And you're trying to pin it on me!"

"I am not the one grubbing for an inheritance," Jarrod growled back. "And it's not my fault that you can't make it on your own. Don't blame me for your failures." He narrowed his eyes. "No one would be looking at you if you could support yourself without your mother-in-law there to give you free rent and bail out your business ventures every two years."

"Hey, shut your mouth!" Jack Francis said.

"Just so you get that you messed this one up yourself," Jarrod scowled as he took a step that put him nose to nose with the younger, shorter man. "You talked too much about your next big step, and then she turned you down. Half the town knows. And they know exactly how mad you were. It's your lack of judgment and your blabbing that got you in trouble, not me."

Jack Francis seemed momentarily taken aback, and Jarrod took advantage of his confusion. "I'm done talking about this," he said, "and you'd better be, too." And with that he walked out with only a quick look at Helen and a sweep of the store that made Po feel as if he'd cataloged the people inside.

In the wake of his exit, Jack Francis turned white and then red again by turns. Then he slammed his fist down on the counter, making all three women jump. Helen, backed against the wall, watched him warily, but said nothing. Finally, he squared his shoulders and strode out. Po watched him hesitate on the sidewalk outside and then head for his Pontiac, which was parked two doors down.

Po returned her attention to the inside of the shop and felt a surge of gratitude toward the salt-and-pepper-haired woman who'd clearly been shopping when the confrontation occurred. She picked up a silver pen to use on the elegant note cards she was carrying and walked up to Helen to check out, saying, "Well, nothing like a little excitement." With this friendly effort toward normalization, Helen managed a nod and a small smile and checked her out, handing her a crisp black-and-white bag with her choices nicely packaged inside.

Just as the woman left, the shop phone rang, and Po watched out of the corner of her eye as Helen took a deep breath and answered it, "Hello, this is The Ink Spot." Clearly it was a personal call. She seemed to recognize the caller's voice immediately, saying, "Well, hi there," with a slightly shaky smile. And then her end of the conversation dropped into short responses, limited to, "Uh huh." "Yes, I know." "OK." "Yes, that sounds good." "Yeah, thanks." And "bye."

Po used this time to look around and think as quickly as she could about the next step. She knew Helen, although not well, and liked her. Selma had created a quilt for the store. It hung on the wall behind the counter. And during the process of working out the design, Helen had often been in Selma's while Po was there. Po had found Helen easygoing and friendly, with a quirky sense of humor. She'd been excited about the quilt, and even hung a small placard next to it, with Selma's name, the name of the piece and a note about the materials.

It was an all-white, whole-cloth quilt, with a delicate feather pen and a scroll of paper stitched in the center. A cable pattern framed the focal point, and then a grid formed of thousands and thousands of tiny stitches filled the background. "Selma did a beautiful job on it," thought Po.

As Helen wrapped up her conversation, Po chose some note cards herself, a set that featured a black-and-white drawing of a woman and her Dalmatian, riding in a red convertible. Even in her hurry to make a choice, the dog spoke to her, nose in the air and ears flying. She chose a dark red pen from the enticing selection of colorful writing utensils and made her way to the counter.

"Hi, Helen," she said with a gentle smile. "Quite a scene. I bet that doesn't happen here often."

Helen laughed, a bit shakily. "No," she agreed. "Maybe I need to hire a bouncer."

Then she sobered. "I really shouldn't make jokes," she said. "Not with what's happening. Poor Mercedes…"

"It's so sad," Po agreed. "And so hard to believe that anyone in Crestwood would harm anyone else."

Helen nodded vigorously. "And the nerve of Jack Francis suggesting that Jarrod had anything to do with her murder. Like he cares about her money. He would never —" In the middle of an angry headshake, she stopped short. And with her next sentence she returned to her normal, business like manner, giving Po the total and taking her credit card, as if nothing extraordinary had happened that morning.

But during the time she stood at the counter, she'd noticed that the tall latte Jarrod had walked down with was sitting right by the register, next to an uneaten muffin. "I wonder…." Po thought. "It could be."

CHAPTER 14

On Thursday morning, Po was just formulating her mental plan for the day, when the phone rang and her plan suddenly changed.

"Hi, Po," Phoebe said. "Do you still want my country club report?"

"Of course," she said. "And even if I didn't, I would never pass up the opportunity to see you."

And with that, they arranged for Phoebe to come by in an hour or so.

"I dropped the boys off with a friend of mine," Phoebe said

when she arrived at the front door. "They adore her son, and they're going to play for a bit, but I can't take too long. It's not easy to herd three boys. At any age. And these three are all 4. That's not a walk in the park, even for an experienced mom."

"You could have brought them," Po said. "It's been too long since I've seen them."

"You're the best, of course," Phoebe said as they settled into the chairs by the fire. Po started a fresh pot of coffee. "But I wanted to be able to just give you my report without my brain being split worrying about what they might be into." Phoebe ran her fingers through her short hair, rumpling it even more, if that were possible. "It's hard to decide where to start," she said. "OK, well … my mother-in-law was thrilled that I showed some interest in the Women's Club, of course. She wishes I would go all the time. And she was all into it because they were doing the planning for their Halloween gala." Phoebe sniffed. "Whatever," she said. "Halloween is the best holiday of the year. Lots of candy. Freedom to enjoy some fantasy. No stuffy family dinner. And that creaky crew wants to go and ruin the whole thing by stealing the theme for a stuffy 'get together.'"

Po smiled and poured Phoebe her piping-hot, rich-smelling coffee. Phoebe really only managed-truce with her stuffy in-laws because of real devotion to her tall-dark-and-handsome lawyer husband. Well, that and being tired of her experience with a lifetime of family conflict. She vowed never to put her beloved little boys in the role of referee that she'd played so often as a child. Still, her free spirit bubbled out. Happily it normally bubbled out in a cheery sort of way.

"So, we arrived right on time, of course. And everybody was standing around in the corners talking about Mercedes' disappearance."

"What were they saying?" Po asked.

"Well, word seems to have leaked that the police are investigating," Phoebe said. "They were mostly getting the stragglers up to speed about how long she'd been gone. And there was some catty commentary thrown in about how many people hated her, but that nasty manners isn't something that generally got you killed. I didn't get to hear much, because they called the meeting to order just a minute or two after we arrived."

Phoebe stopped a moment, and looked intently at Po. "But really, none of that is the interesting part."

"Well," Po said with some surprise, "get to the interesting part then."

"Well, I went to the bathroom during the social period. I worried at the time that I'd miss something key. All the talking during the meeting was dull, and I was sure there was going to be some good information exchanged sometime."

Po thought she might be overly optimistic, having been to many women's meetings in her day, but she didn't want to interrupt.

"But I had, had, had to go," Phoebe said. "I've been really trying to get the recommended 64 ounces of water a day, you know. And I took a wrong turn on my way back. I got about halfway the wrong direction up the hall, and I heard people talking in one of the rooms."

"What were they talking about?" Po asked. "Could you tell?"

"I wasn't sure at first," Phoebe said. "I stopped because it sounded like a woman was in trouble. I heard a thump, and she kind of shrieked. I thought at first he'd hit her."

"Who'd hit her?" Po said, suddenly concerned.

"I think it was Jack Francis," Phoebe said. "But I didn't guess that until later. And he didn't really hit her. I think he smacked a table or the wall or something. But for sure he scared her. I think they heard me, because they stopped talking. I must have made a noise."

"But before that, they sounded really intense," Phoebe went on. "I couldn't really hear what they were saying. But then I heard the woman say, "Don't you threaten me!" And it was right after that that I heard the smack."

"But you're sure he didn't hit her?" Po asked.

"Pretty sure," Phoebe said. "But then I was really close. And I heard him say, 'You'd better be more careful, or you're going to have something more serious to worry about than the life of a dog. Like your own well-being.' And then I scuttled, because I was thought they'd find me there."

"And a good thing, too," Po reassured her. "You needed to get out of there. I would never forgive myself for putting you into danger."

"I'm not sure who the woman was," Phoebe said. "I didn't notice anyone else missing from the meeting, but there were at least 30 people there. I'm sure I'm not the only one who took a bathroom break along the way. But on the way in, I had noticed that there was a young guy taking care of the valet parking. At the time I was thinking all those gals were pretty spoiled if they couldn't even park their own cars. Here's the key, though." Phoebe spoke with an intensity that Po could easily feel. "On the way out, the valet pulled up in a red Pontiac GTO. And Kate said that's what Jack Francis drives. I kind of hung out, dropped my keys once and fumbled around and stuff trying to make sure, and he walked right out."

She looked at Po. "That sure makes it seem like it was him, right?"

"It could have been," Po agreed.

"And he was threatening someone!" she insisted.

"Well, it does seem like it," Po said.

"But you're not completely sold," Phoebe said with some apparent let down.

"I don't think we can lock him up and throw away the key," Po said apologetically. "But it's sure going to give me something to think about. On the downside, we don't know who he was talking to. And they have a lot of dogs. Even if we can prove it was him, we can't probably prove that he was talking about Fitzgerald."

"Maybe you're right," Phoebe said. "I may be having delusions of grandeur. I dream about bringing you the fact that busts the case wide open and frees my dear friend Maggie from suspicion."

"You did a great job," Po reassured her. "I appreciate your sacrifices for the investigation."

"I really was a bit frightened," Phoebe admitted. "They sounded so serious. I really thought he might hurt her."

"And he might have," Po agreed. "He might have."

"Here's the last thing," Phoebe said. "I'm not sure it's

important, but I did ask around a little about the benefit for the humane society. I figured if Mercedes was running that, she'd be getting her golf-club cohorts involved somehow. And I was right, I guess. One of the women said she heard that Mercedes had booked the bed and breakfast with Adele for the event. And she said if she hadn't already disappeared, Adele might have killed her. I asked what she meant, and all she'd say is that Mercedes had yanked Adele's chain past the point of choking her."

Po and Phoebe knew Adele fairly well. She had commissioned eight quilts from the Queen Bees for her bed and breakfast. And during the project, the Bees had solved her brother's murder. "It's not that tough to yank Adele's chain, if you remember," Po said.

"We came out on her good side," Phoebe said with a shrug. "I guess clearing someone of murder and keeping the whole town from turning against her should have some small rewards."

"Do you know what she did to make Adele so mad?" Po asked.

Phoebe laughed. "Can you imagine those two in a room?" she asked. "I imagine they were both fairly het up before it was over."

"No details?" asked Po again.

"Oh, right," Phoebe said. "Details. I think the main issue was about the menu and who would cater. I think Adele only works with certain caterers, and Mercedes demanded someone else." She gave Po a mischievous smile. "It couldn't have been pretty."

Phoebe looked at Po inquiringly. "Do you think someone like that who worked with Mercedes on a particular project could get mad enough to kidnap her. Or a groomer? Or a prospective puppy buyer? Or a former doggie foster parent? You know, I only met her a few times, but I can see how she might rub people the wrong way."

Po smiled. "She sure could be demanding. And I think anything's a possibility right now. I'll have to think about how all the pieces might fit."

"OK," Phoebe said, gathering up her bag and phone and jacket. "I know you're better qualified for thinking than I am," she laughed. "It's been literally years since I have had a moment to think. And it's time to go collect my two little brain suckers."

She gave Po a quick hug.

"I know you'll figure out how to help Aaron and Maggie," she said. "You're our solution finder."

Po smiled at Phoebe, and as she watched her go, she felt a momentary twinge for those days when she was the center of her children's universe. That was such a fulfilling time. She missed the smell of warm baby after bath, lanky grade-school-aged arms around her neck, and finding stray Barbie shoes everywhere.

Then her mind returned instead to the goings on in Phoebe's country club world and she felt instead cold fear. She must talk to Kate.

She dialed her cell phone. No response. "That's not really a surprise," she told herself. "She's probably in class." Still, she couldn't shake the feeling that Kate needed to be warned. "She just can't go following Jack Francis around," Po thought. "And she won't give up easily. Still, short of going to track her down, there's nothing I can do now," Po thought. She left a message for Kate to call, and closed her phone.

Stymied for the moment, she thought about what more she could do to gather information. If it wasn't Aaron who killed Mercedes, "and that can't be, I refuse to believe it," she thought, "it could be Jarrod. It could be Jack Francis. It could be anyone," she thought with despair. "What I need is more information!"

With her mind whirling, she revisited all the paths she'd pursued so far. Where could she make progress? Learn more? And she dialed Eleanor.

Gracious as always, Eleanor invited her to come by and offered her lunch when she arrived. Po hadn't realized she was even hungry until she smelled the creamy tomato soup. But the rich, warm taste of it made her gratefully sigh as she took the first bite. "This is wonderful, Eleanor," she said.

"It's one of my favorites," Eleanor agreed. "It's made with sun-dried tomatoes, so I can have it all winter if I want. Comfort food."

And indeed it was, particularly with a side of aged cheddar and crackers. The two friends settled in companionably to talk about what they'd learned in the last 24 hours.

"Well, Mike was on the story, for sure, when I met with him last night," Eleanor said. "There's a piece in the paper today." She got up and brought a copy of the local paper to Po, and then she sat quietly eating, and Po skimmed it.

"No mention of Maggie's clinic yet," she said, looking slightly relieved.

"It's probably just a matter of time," Eleanor said matter of factly. "He knew they'd searched the clinic yesterday."

"Mercedes is a pretty prominent in Crestwood," Po acknowledged. "There was bound to be coverage of her disappearance."

"That's the other thing," Eleanor said. "They covered it in the article as a disappearance, but not as a homicide. The Police Department is trying to keep that bit quiet so the press coverage doesn't interfere with their investigation."

"We can't just sit around and wait for more bad press," Po said. "Maggie is so stressed. I'm not sure I've ever seen her like this. And poor Aaron. I'm not sure he realizes how serious this could be."

"I did ask Mike to let me know when they were printing any new developments," Eleanor said. "He owes me a favor, so I think he will."

"Well, that's good," Po said. "At least we won't be caught off-guard."

"And there's one more thing," Eleanor said. "He said that we should ask more questions about the car. But he wouldn't say why." She sniffed. "Those news reporters and their off-the-record hints. Ridiculous."

"Interesting," Po said. "Maybe we can find out more."

"Hey," Eleanor said. "Since I have you here. Come and look at my latest project."

The two went upstairs to Eleanor's airy workroom. She

had boxes of fabrics in clear plastic containers lining one set of bookshelves at the north end. On her worktable lay at least 100 half-inch strips of fabric, along with 15 or 20 ribbons.

"I'm playing with stripes, clearly," Eleanor said with a laugh.

"I love it," Po smiled. "Totally fun. I like the polka dots particularly well. How big are you thinking the finished piece will be?"

"Not too big," Eleanor said. "Maybe 14 inches wide and about 24 long. At least that's what I'm playing with."
Po looked more closely at the strips that Eleanor had in place.   "This diagonal black-and-white piece is really doing a lot for me," she said.

"Me, too," Eleanor said. "It was when I laid that one down that I started to think I might be on the right track." She looked at Po. "That's one of my favorite parts of any project," she said. "That moment when you feel the pieces start to become a whole."

"I know exactly what you mean," Po said. "And sometimes it seems like that moment takes a long time to come."

Eleanor laughed. "You guys sure challenged me with that cat square. I had to redo the ears on mine half a dozen times before I thought they worked."

"Really?" Po said. "Your cat was darling. I loved it."

Eleanor's pieced cat square had featured a saucy looking, fluffy cat with a "just ate the canary" satisfaction about her.

"I really do have a special spot in my heart for cats," Eleanor said. "It has been years since I've had one of my own. But I love their independent spirit."

"That reminds me," Po said. "I've been wondering what role, exactly, Mercedes was filling for the humane society benefit. We need to figure out if we should fill in for her on any duties."

"I'll ask around," Eleanor said, "and let you know what I learn."

"OK," Po said. "I'll do anything you need, of course."

Home at last, Po decided she was out of ideas and out of steam and she lay down for a nap. She used to nap every day, when her kids were young, and when she did, she was fond of quoting the benefits of napping to any and all who would listen. But she'd gotten out of the habit. Still, today a small recharging of her batteries seemed a must.

She fell instantly asleep, that deep sleep that leaves you unsure of your surroundings, and she woke with a start to the sound of her phone ringing. "That's what I get for getting out of practice," she grumbled to herself as she fumbled around, trying to locate it. "I'm nap-whacky."

"Po?"

"Yes?"

"It's Kate," she said, sounding a little surprised at needing to identify herself.

"Sorry, sweet," Po said, sitting down on the arm of the sofa and trying to wrest her fuzzy brain back into focus. "I'm with you now."

"You left me a message to call?" Kate said.

"Yes, I did," Po said, and she recounted her conversation with Phoebe and her eventful afternoon at the Crestwood

Dog-Gone Murder

shops. "You must be more careful," Po said. "I would never forgive myself if I let you put yourself in danger."

"I haven't used up my nine lives yet," Kate said. "And it sounds like you've been living more dangerously than I have by far."

"Really, Kate," Po said.

"I know, Po," Kate said. "But I've been careful. Subtle, even, and you know that takes some effort on my part."

"So what have you been up to?" Po asked.

"Well, first I went down to the hardware store," Kate said. "I shopped for a new chain for my bike. You have to agree that's plausible."

Po smiled. "Yes, OK. Moderately subtle."

"While I was there, I talked to the old guy that owns the store a bit. Asked if he'd been busy. Asked if he really kept live bait in that cooler with the fruit juices. He brought up Jarrod on his own, once we hit the topic of fishing."

"OK, that's pretty good," Po said. "You're getting better at subtlety, I think."

"Damning with faint praise, I see," Kate said. "Moving on, he did confirm that he saw Jarrod on the same day that Mercedes disappeared."

"I did tell you that," Po pointed out.

"I know, but still. It doesn't hurt to do a little legwork. I just wanted to see if I could learn any more."

"And did you?" Po asked.

"He said Jarrod was a regular. Angela is right—he goes fishing a lot," Kate said. "That means that he probably doesn't have an alibi for the time when Mercedes was killed."

"He could have been seen by another fisherman," Po pointed out. "Or maybe coming back into town with a fish, or something."

"I'm just saying that he's still in the running," Kate said. "His story is not any better than Aaron's, for sure."

"OK," Po said. "Agreed. Did you learn anything else?"

"I also wandered back by the dealership," Kate said. "I told them that I had run into some unexpected expenses, so I wasn't really in the market this second. But I had to come and dream a little. They seemed to buy that."

Po laughed. "I'm sure you were very convincing," she said. "You always were. Especially when you wanted something."

"I wanted information," Kate said. "And I did get a little. I eventually brought up Jack Francis causally. I said I'd seen the newspaper item, and how terrible it must be for him. The guy told me I shouldn't feel that bad because Jack Francis would be rich when this was all over."

"Really?" Po said. "I wouldn't have expected that."

"Me neither," Kate said. "So then I asked if the police had been out asking questions."

"What did he say?"

"No. But he said they'd talked to Jack Francis at the house. Apparently he came into the dealership all steamed about it the next day."

She paused, and Po sensed her excitement.

"Here's the good part," Kate said finally. "Jack Francis was not at the dealership when Mercedes disappeared. And we know he was not at home, either. So he was missing in action, too. And guess what the guy said?"

Dog-Gone Murder

"What?" Po obliged.

"He said, 'And if I were the one in charge of this investigation, I would be taking a close look at where he was. That man has too much to gain and too much to lose right now.'"

"Wow," Po said.

"Exactly," Kate came back. "Can you believe it?"

"He may not know anything," Po tried to warn herself and Kate.

"Yes, I know," Kate said. "But he could be right, too. And right now I'm just looking for people with motive and opportunity who are not Aaron. I'm not exactly finding them in short supply."

Po had to smile. "You have been busy," she said. "Good work. You're amazing. But please," she said, remembering her worries from the morning. "Please, no more investigating. You've done your part."

"You're just worried I'll get into trouble," Kate said.

"Of course I am," Po responded. "Your mom was my best friend. She would never understand. I promised to watch out for you."

"I've gotta run," Kate said. "I promise to behave myself for the next few hours. Maybe we can confer in the morning. I have the day off work. And I need help deciding the next step."

"OK," Po said, happy to extract a promise of quiet caution, even if it was temporary. "Let me think and plot and plan. Come by in the morning and we can talk again."

And with that the two said goodbye and Kate headed for her evening, flush with the successes of the day.

Po, however, continued to worry. About Kate. About Maggie. About Aaron. About what this violence meant for her haven of a town. And about what to do next.

To ease her out-of-sync body and her uncomfortable state of mind, Po started manufacturing her one sure fix for relaxation and re-energizing: a small pot of strong cinnamon tea. The aroma filled the whole kitchen and seemed to settle around her warmly. She was settled in a deep comfortable chair working on her second cup of brewed spice and the continuation of her furious contemplation when the phone rang again.

"Maggie," she said, much more alert for this call. " Are you done for the day?"

"Done for is more like it," she said. "And yet, no. We're just taking a break. Then I'm taking Maya to dinner. But I wanted to call and check in."

"Oh, I'm glad you did," Po said. "I was hoping to hear how it went. But maybe that will have to wait until tomorrow."

"The full blown version will, I think," Maggie said. "But I think it's going fine. Maya is smart. I'm glad to have her helping me. By the end, I think I'll have a plan."

"That always makes me feel better," Po said. "The problem doesn't have to be fixed. I just need to know my next step."

"Exactly," Maggie said. "Speaking of next steps, how's that other problem going? You know, the one with the dead woman at the center? Did you learn anything with my crew today?"

"I have a few questions for you," Po said, "but nothing earth-shattering. We're still working, though. Kate's doing some more digging. We should know more by tomorrow."

"Maybe we could have dinner tomorrow night," Po went on. "I know Max would like to hear how it went. And I could gather the troops to make reports."

"That sounds perfect, Po," Maggie said. "I'll be there. I need to get some more steps down the road on all these problems—before they get any worse."

"I know, Maggie. I feel bad about all this," Po said.

"I'm trying not to let things get blown out of proportion," Maggie said. "But any more weeks like this one, and I could be ruined. Out of business. My life's dream down the tubes."

"That's not going to happen, Maggie. It just can't."

"Well, I'll go to dinner. Take the next step. Get a good night's sleep. We'll tackle it again tomorrow," Maggie said, with a trace of her normal joviality. "Tomorrow's a new day. It will get better. Or I could change course and be a dog walker." She gave a short laugh and said her goodbyes.

"We won't let it happen," Po said to her now silent phone. "I couldn't bear it."

Hoover seemed to nod in agreement. And then he plumped up the couch cushion and went back to sleep.

"I wish I shared your confidence," Po said with a slight frown at her lounging pet.

Given that she'd taken a fairly healthy siesta, Po found herself with unusual energy for the end of her day. She sat down with the copies of the appointment book and thumbed through them once. Nothing. All that information, and yet nothing that seemed to help her situation. She started again, this time just looking at the totals spent. Some were higher, some lower. Again, nothing seemed to relate to Mercedes or her disappearance.

Po sat for a moment staring at the pile of papers. Then she reviewed one more time, just looking at who'd visited. Almost right away she found Jack Francis was on the list of clients, not once but three times. And a couple of pages later she found Mercedes listed. And Jack Francis again. And Mercedes again. And again. "Maggie did say Mercedes was her biggest spending client," Po said to Hoover, who managed to lift one heavy eyelid and cock one lazy ear her way. "But I guess I didn't realize how often she'd be visiting."

Near the end of the sheaf of papers, she found her own name right next to Mercedes', a record of that fateful day when Aaron found himself facing Mercedes' wrath. "Who'd have ever thought one crabby cat could lead to such a big mess," Po thought.

She sat for one more moment thinking, and then totaled up how much Mercedes and Jack Francis had spent over their visits in the month. "I guess Maggie might know whether this is typical," she thought. And she bundled up the papers and piled them on the kitchen table to talk about later.

Next she popped a chicken and some potatoes in the oven to roast and put a bottle of wine in the fridge to chill. And with dinner going, she went back to her studio room to focus on her writing for the hour remaining before Max arrived.

The sound of Max's gentle knock as he opened the door was

a welcome reprieve from her computer screen, and she went to greet him with a smile.

"You look wonderful," he said, leaning in to give her a kiss.

"Thank you," Po said, enjoying, as always, his open appreciation.

"Now," he said. "Are you staying out of trouble?" He was smiling, but Po knew he was serious. And, she had to admit, she'd gotten herself in a couple of tight spots during the time he'd known her. But, she thought, this was different.

"Of course," she said, smiling back. "I have offered Maggie some moral support during this challenging time. But that's all."

"So, you and Kate aren't teaming up on some detective work on the side?" he asked, one eyebrow raised.

"Detective work?" Po asked slowly.

"Yes," he said firmly. "Snooping. Prying. Excessive questions about things that police officers are looking into. Detective work."

Po didn't answer, choosing instead to lead Max into the kitchen.

"I think dinner's about ready," she said. "Would you pour the wine?"

"Sure," he said. "But I did still notice the sidestepping."

She turned to face him. "I'm just helping my friend," she said earnestly. "You would do the same thing."

His face softened as he looked down on her. "You may be right," he said. "But you plow into these things as though you think you're invincible." He ran one finger along her set jaw.

"And Kate is just as bad or worse. Please, be careful."

"I will be," she promised. "Kate and I will be very careful."

"I wish I believed that," he said.

C H A P T E R 1 5

Po got up in the morning, threw on a lounging-around suit of emerald green velour, and started a pot of coffee. Then she quickly mixed a batch of easy drop biscuits, one of Kate's favorites. She sat by the sliding glass doors, thinking and drinking her coffee. And she was just pulling the biscuits out of the oven when Kate knocked gently and came in.

"You're the best," she said, sniffing the warm, welcoming aroma of the freshly baked treats and pouring herself a cup of Po's rich coffee and adding a healthy dose of warm milk. She gave Po a little squeeze, and then retrieved some small plates and napkins from the cupboard while Po put the biscuits on a platter and got out the butter and a jar of smooth blackberry jelly, her favorite.

"So, did you have time to think?" Kate asked as she dug into the flaky treat.

"I want you to look at something with me," Po said.

She opened the laptop she'd positioned within comfortable reach and launched her picture viewer to display a set of photos. "I took these on the day after the police came to Maggie's clinic," she said. "I thought we could look at them. Maybe it will spark something for us."

"Great idea," Kate said, wiping her hands on a napkin and reaching for the computer. "And you were brilliant that you thought to take the camera."

"As my expert advisor on both photography and police procedure, you seemed like the perfect person to review them," Po said, smiling.

Kate expertly maneuvered through the folder, frowning with concentration, her head tilted to one side and her coffee forgotten for the moment.

Po sat quietly, just watching as Kate reviewed every shot. "You took a lot," she said when she finished. "I need to look at them again." She ate another biscuit, and then repeated the whole process, squinting at each and every picture a second time. Finally she pushed the laptop back to the middle of the table and looked at Po.

"Well, what do you think?" Po said. "Do you see anything out of the ordinary?"

"You took pictures of all the areas that it looked as though the police paid special attention to, right?" Kate asked.

"Yes," Po confirmed. "But it's hard to know for sure what they looked at, unless Maggie saw them or they left things disrupted. So then I just tried to take whatever I could think of."

Kate thought for a moment.

"Did Maggie look at these?"

"No," Po said. "But she said she didn't notice anything unusual around the clinic either before or after the police had come."

"So," Kate said slowly, "If there's something unusual here, it doesn't look out of place to the people who know it best." She took another biscuit and ate it slowly.

"Did you notice anything in the pictures, Po?" she asked finally.

"No," Po admitted.

She got up and refilled both their coffee cups, and the two drank coffee in silence for a moment.

Kate finally sighed. "It seems smart to have taken the pictures. But I've got nothing here."

"Thanks for trying," Po said gently. She was a little disappointed.

"You gave me an idea, though," Kate said a little more brightly. "What we need is more information. And photos are great for that."

She got up with energy. "You've taken pictures of the clinic. I'm going to go hit other sites of interest. Mercedes' house, the dealership. Maybe we'll notice something when we look at those."

Kate agreed to bring P.J. back for dinner and headed out.

After she left, Po called Leah to get her up to speed and get advice on the plan for the next day.

"Kate is right," Leah said with authority. "We need more information. Where better to go than as close to the source as possible?"

Po was still not completely convinced that visiting the Richardsons' house was a completely safe, well-thought-through option. But she couldn't disagree that it might be the next logical step.

"Taking food is always the right thing," Leah said. "We can go together. With two heads, maybe we'll ask some good questions and learn something."

They agreed to go the next day, after the Queen Bees assembled.

"I hope this is a good idea," Po said to Hoover.

He looked at her with a quizzical expression.

"I just have a bad feeling about it," she said in answer.

It was something of a tradition for Po to find a way to fill her house with people on Friday night. She cooked for a crowd and was rarely disappointed. This week seemed to be no exception. The door swung open at a bit before 6, when Maggie arrived.

"So, how did it go with the consultant?" Po asked, when they'd both found a comfortable seat and a pleasing beverage.

"I think it went well," Maggie said, letting out something of a sigh. "She really helped me focus on where the problem might be."

Like what?" Po asked, taking a sip of her signature drink,

a beautiful ice cold martini with a delicate slice of apple floating on the top. "I keep hoping there's a quick fix."

"Well, nothing overnight. But I feel better because I know what the next steps are, at least. And we ruled out a bunch of things."

"Really?" Po asked, taking a heavily laden piece of bruschetta.

"Yeah," Maggie said. "My problem really could only be revenue that's too low or expenses that are too high. And there are really not that many things that fuel revenue. So we looked at those today. I see about an average number of new clients each month. So that's not the problem."

"Well, it's nice to cross something off the list," Po smiled.

Maggie gave her a wry smile in return. "Unfortunately I feel a little like I do about weight loss," she said. "The formula is very simple. Eat less; move more. But it's still not that easy for me to do." She frowned a little at the hors d'oeuvre she was eating. And then she shrugged and took another bite.

"Well, what is it exactly that you have to do?" Po asked.

Maggie took a small sip of the fragrant wine. "I have to adjust my fees, for one," she said. "I haven't bothered for a couple of years." She made a face. "It's not really my favorite thing to think about. But Maya is right, my expenses have gone up. So I have to adjust."

Po nodded. "That makes sense. And it doesn't seem that bad, really."

"Yeah, I know," Maggie said. "I also need to do a better job reminding clients to come back in for the care their pets need. Right now, we sort of expect them to keep track and call when they're out of medication or when it's time to do tests. But given how busy people are, that's probably not realistic."

Po nodded again. "So, you're happy about it over all, right?" she asked.

Maggie nodded. "Yeah," she said. "You know, I didn't apply to veterinary school because I wanted to own a business," she said. "I just wanted to help pets. But I can't do that unless the business is running well. I need to be able to pay the electric company and my team and buy equipment and supplies." She sighed again. "It has taken me 15 years, but I think I finally get it. I need to work on my business, and not just in it."

Po laughed. "You make it sound so bad," she said. "You deserve to be successful. And you'll be great at the business side, if that's what you decide to do," she said. "You've always been able to do anything you set your mind to."

Maggie seemed to cheer up a little. "You're right," she said. "This is all about my attitude. So that means I can fix it."

"So," Po said, "I know you have a million things on your mind and a bucket load of clients to see, since you've been busy with Maya. But do you think you could fit in a quick meeting with your team? I think they'd benefit from a five-minute recap of your consultant's recommendations."

"Well, sure," Maggie said. "I was going to wait until we had a little more time to talk about it. But I could do it sooner."

"I don't mean to meddle," Po said. "But it came out in the little talks I did that they're worried you may cut back on staffing."

Maggie laughed. "I should have known," she said. "We all see the problem from our own perspective, don't we? I like those easy-to-fix issues. I'll let them know that no one's getting fired this week."

Then her pep seemed to fade a little again.

"Of course, I've got a couple of other problems," she said. "I've been closed up in an office for two days. Is there any news about Mercedes. I mean, I know I'd have heard if she'd been found, but are the police making any progress?"

Po caught Maggie up, with a review of Phoebe's report, what she'd learned about Jack Francis, Po's own concerns about Jarrod. She finished with an account of the outing with Aaron and the rope they'd found.

"Aaron says Fitzgerald had a rope around his neck when Aaron found him," Po explained to Maggie. "And if he'd been tied up, that certainly makes it seem certain that he was taken and not that he found a way out or was unintentionally freed."

"I agree," Maggie said thoughtfully. "I'll ask him about it again tomorrow," Maggie said decisively. "And I'll talk to him about what Angela said about the food."

She sighed. "I like him. I don't want to believe he'd ever do anything to hurt the clinic. But I have to be realistic, too. I have too much invested in my practice to be sentimental if someone I trust doesn't deserve that faith."

"I feel the same way," Po said. "I really like him. But you have to be clear-minded about this. Get to the bottom of it." She paused. "I'm sure he'll put all your worries to rest," she said, trying to be reassuring.

"I hope so, too, Po," Maggie said. "But we'll see."

A few minutes later, Po felt the familiar burst of pleasure when she saw Kate walk through the door, and she was just as pleased to see her goddaughter had P.J. in tow.

"It's been forever since you've been over," she said, giving him a hug.

"A couple of weeks, at least," he said, laughing. "But I'm glad you missed me."

Po set out round two of her snacks, a big tray of fresh veggies and dip. Max arrived on the heels of Kate and P.J. and started pouring wine for the newcomers, and the talk naturally turned to the trials Maggie was facing and the latest developments.

"Maggie," Po said slowly. "The police seemed awfully interested in the drug log. What would they be looking for there?"

"We use all kinds of restricted drugs," Maggie said. "Just like human physicians. But many practices don't have very tight security measures."

"But you do?" Po asked.

"I'm not saying no one could ever leave with anything," Maggie said. "But we know the rules and follow them."

"What kind of rules?" Po asked.

"Well, controlled substances must be stored in a locked drawer or cabinet. And you have to limit access to authorized members of the team. When you use a controlled substance, you have to note the date, the amount you used, the amount remaining in the container, the animal receiving the drug, and your name."

"What drugs are most likely to be targeted?" Po asked.

"Ketamine might be the biggest lure for a thief," Maggie said. "People have broken into practices to steal it in the United States, although it tends to happen more in Mexico. It used to be used more in human medicine, but it causes hallucinations."

"Nice to avoid that if you can," Max commented, dryly.

"Exactly. When it's stolen, it's either injected or the liquid is evaporated until it makes a white powder, which is snorted." Po looked at her wide-eyed, and Maggie laughed at her surprise. "We hear right away when a clinic's been hit," she said. "The veterinary journals have done a good job informing us about the thefts and the drugs' uses."

"What other controlled drugs do you keep on hand?" Po asked.

"We have about 10," Maggie said. "Many of them you wouldn't recognize. But we have morphine, pentobarbital, euthanasia solution, of course."

"Not that long ago, Illinois police broke up a drug ring that was targeting veterinary clinics," P.J. chimed in.

"Really?" Po asked.

"Uh, huh. They were stealing ketamine. And there wasn't anyone in the group who was older than 20," he said. "One boy in the group said he was making up to $2,000 a week selling the drug."

"Who would he be selling to?" Max asked. "Other kids?"

"Mostly," P.J. said. "Ketamine is a popular club drug. It can be injected, smoked, swallowed, or snorted. Mostly they prefer injection, because it burns your nasal passages if you snort it. And it tastes terrible. But it will make you high."

"I had no idea," Po said.

"You haven't been very into the club scene lately," P.J. teased.

"Is it dangerous?" Po asked.

"The high doesn't last long. An hour or less. And it's tough to overdose. The lethal limit is many times the standard dosage," P.J. said. "And then you would just pass out."

"Are other drugs commonly stolen from veterinarians?" Max asked.

"Ketamine is the most common," P.J. said. "But I did do a little digging in the archive. There are also reports of a practice that had euthanasia solution stolen in a break-in. I think that had to have been a case worthy of the Darwin awards."

"What's that?" Po asked.

"Stupid theft. Dumb enough you'd laugh. What would you ever do with euthanasia solution?" P.J. said. "You'd go into a coma long before you got high."

"Truly not bright," Kate said, rejoining them after a sojourn to the kitchen to check the roast and baked potatoes. "Ready to eat?"

And with that, talk of overdoses and theft was abandoned, at least for the moment. But it left Po with things to think about for hours after they'd all gone. Disagreeable thoughts, for certain. Surely Aaron couldn't be stealing food from the clinic. Or drugs. It was just impossible. Wasn't it?

CHAPTER 16

It was with a sense of life being unsettled that Po gathered up the tote bag that she reserved for Queen Bees meetings and headed down to Selma's store. Too many problems. The mystery of Fitzgerald's disappearance unsolved. Mercedes abduction and likely murder. The suspicion falling on Aaron. And Maggie's financial problems. Usually she'd be feeling at her most calm with the prospect of three hours with the Bees ahead. But today she couldn't even get focused enough to figure out what to put in her bag to work on.

When she arrived at Parker's Dry Goods she sensed that she was not the only one who was suffering disquiet. She was running a little late, and the rest of the Bees had arrived and were chatting quietly. But the dynamic seemed off. Tense. Instead of engaging in their normal chatter about ongoing projects, their lives, and their news, the Bees seemed quiet. Watchful.

"Oh, good," Selma said when she saw Po taking off the lined rust-colored rain jacket she'd put on to ward off the chill of the October morning. "You're here."

The other quilters stopped talking and turned to her.

"Maggie said we had to wait for you to get an update," Selma said.

"I know I'm at the center of this maelstrom," Maggie said. "But you're the acting information hub. I wanted you to be here to help me sort out where we are and what's going on in some coherent way."

With nods at points from the participants along the way, Maggie and Po, with occasional help from Kate, tried to tell the story. They started with the interruption the week before when Aaron had come by the Queen Bees meeting to say the dog was gone, and then followed the trail through the finding of Fitzgerald, his return, and Mercedes' disappearance.

"We've had so much difficulty and disruption lately," Selma said, looking at Maggie with sympathy. "It seems like the perfect day for us to share something wonderful."

She went around the corner, and came back with a pieced quilt top over one arm. Susan helped her hold it up, with their backs to the group. Then they circled around so everyone could see. It was their fundraiser quilt top, their individual squares pieced together into a whole, a process that Po always felt was somehow magical.

"It looks awesome," Phoebe said, speaking for all of them.

"It does," agreed Eleanor. "You did an incredible job piecing it, Selma."

"You did, of course," Kate said with a laugh. "But there's still a lot of work to be done. Can we really get it done by next weekend?"

"Well, we knew it would be tight," Susan said. "I've cleared my schedule as much as I can. And I think I can get it quilted over the next three or four days. I just have to stay really focused. Then Po said she'd do the binding."

"Luckily it's not too big," Selma said.

They all nodded.

"Can I come by tomorrow and help with the quilting?" Phoebe said. "I would really like to do some of it. And if I came here, you'd be around to help me if I run into trouble. I don't have nearly your experience—and I'd like to learn."

"Sure, I'd love some help," Susan said.

The group moved on to talking about how they'd like the piece quilted, and confirmed their earlier choice of backing and binding fabrics. With the key decisions made, they scattered, feeling the joy of creating something together, even given the dark cloud they found themselves under.

Po and Leah left together, carrying out the plan from the day before. They each contributed a container of homemade soup, and they stopped by Marla's and bought a long loaf of seven-grain bread. Leah had brought along a large brown paper tote, and some tissue, and they packaged the food in the bag and headed for the Richardson home. As they trudged up the driveway to the door, Po felt some nervousness kick in. "I wonder if anyone is even home," she said.

"If not, we'll just come back later," Leah assured her.

But someone did open the door. And maybe the perfect someone. The young, slightly round frame of Melanie Richardson appeared, as elegantly dressed as her mother always was, although without the same strength of presence.

"Hi, Melanie," Leah said in response to her somewhat questioning greeting. "I'm sure you don't remember me, but I had you in class a number of years ago, and Po and I were friends of your mother's." Melanie nodded, and Po felt encouraged.

"We wanted to bring this by," she said. "We've sure been thinking about you."

"Why, thank you," Melanie said. "Won't you come in for a moment?"

She brought out a pitcher of iced tea and some glasses, and they settled on the sofa across the coffee table from their hostess. Po noticed she looked drawn and tired. "To be expected," she thought.

"We're both members of a quilting group," she said, "and everyone in our group has some connection to your mom. She was very active in Crestwood; such a social woman and generous with her time."

"Yes, she has always been very involved," Melanie agreed. She thought for a moment. "Isn't Dr. Maggie part of your group?"

"Yes," Leah admitted. "She'd have come with us, but she

was worried that might upset you."

"I can see that," Melanie said. "But I can't believe she'd knowingly hurt Fitz, or let him be hurt. And I can't imagine how the two incidences could be connected." She shrugged. "That the police's problem to figure out," she said.

"I'm sure they're working on it," Po tried to reassure her.

"I hope you're right," Melanie said with a slight frown. "All I've seen them do so far is make a mess of our house. And they've talked with the three of us for hours. And the housekeeper. And the guy who helps with the yard." She shrugged. "I wouldn't be surprised to learn they tried to interview each of the dogs."

Leah laughed. "I've had times I've wished dogs could talk, for sure," she said.

"Maggie did ask us to find out if you're managing with the dogs alright," Po spoke up. "She said she'd be happy to find someone to help if you need it."

Melanie seemed to think it over. "That's very kind," she said finally. "I'll let her know if we decide that would help."

The two women, sensing that was their signal to leave stood up. "We don't want to keep you," Leah said. "We just wanted to express our sympathy."

Melanie showed them to the door, and they walked back toward Leah's car.

When they stepped off the front porch, Po looked at Leah, started to speak, and then shut her mouth again. Leah smiled at her, understanding precisely, and they headed for the car. This was not a good time to get caught saying anything you wouldn't want everyone to hear. And it turned out she'd made a good choice.

"What are you doing here?"

Po and Leah spun around to look.

Jarrod was leaning against the side of the garage, watching them.

"Checking up on me?" He glowered.

"Of course not," Po said.

"You were in the shop the other day," he said accusingly.

"Yes," she admitted.

"And you're friends with the vet."

"Yes," she said again. "But it's not—"

"Well, you're not going to find anything," he said, moving forward threateningly. "Even if I did let you roam around on my property." He took another step in their direction. "And I'm certainly not going to allow that."

He moved even closer, and Po felt her heart pounding in her chest.

"Let me show you to your car," he suggested coldly, and they could feel his anger roll over them in waves as they mutely moved down the driveway.

Po couldn't resist looking back toward the house as they went around the corner, although she tried to be as casual as possible, and he was standing still in the driveway, watching their progress.

"That didn't go that well," she said.

"It didn't go that badly either," Leah said.

Po looked at her with surprise.

Leah saw her look and shrugged. "Neither of us is bruised

or beaten, right?" she said. "We did get to talk with Melanie. And we certainly seem to have confirmed that Jarrod is a top suspect." She thought for a moment. "A worried top suspect, I'd say."

Po watched the familiar streets of Crestwood slide by and thought how uncomfortably foreign this feeling of fear felt in her dear town. "I guess you're right," she said.

"What do we know about him?" Leah asked. "Where was he when Mercedes disappeared?"

"I did see him that day," Po said. "He was going fishing. I met him while he was buying bait. Kate went and chatted up the owner of the hardware store, to see if she could learn more. He confirmed that Jarrod bought bait, but that was all."

"Well, if he was fishing alone, he may not be able to prove where he was during the time she disappeared." She paused. "So then," she picked up her line of thought again. "What did he have to gain?"

Po hesitated. "Mercedes could be hard to live with," she said.

"I have to agree with that," Leah said wryly.

"I think he might have been spending some time with Helen," Po said slowly.

"Really?" Leah asked. "You never said that."

"Well, I can't be sure," Po said. "But if they were having an affair, that could give him some motivation." She paused. "He has always seemed so nice, though. I hate to think it." Leah sniffed. "Did that seem nice to you?" she gestured back the way they'd come.

"No," Po admitted. "But he has been under a lot of stress."

"You always believe the best about people," Leah said.

She looked over at Po and smiled. "It's one of your fine points, of course."

She went back to thinking for a minute.

"What about money?" Po said, finally. "I always heard that marrying Mercedes set him up for life. Is that true?"

"I don't know for sure," Leah said. "But I've heard it, too."

"If it is true," Po said, "he could be our murderer."

CHAPTER 17

On Sunday, Po lived her absolutely normal life. No indication that she was in the midst of terrible chaos, except for her unsettled state of mind. She ran and had a quiet breakfast with Leah, during which they avoided the topics of murder and mayhem. She worked on her landscape. She read the paper and drank coffee. She walked Hoover and cooked a quiet dinner with Max. She could almost believe the dread she seemed to carry with her was a figment of her imagination. The next   day it all became real again.

"You'll never believe it," Maggie said. "Melanie called me

today. She actually wants to take me up on the offer to find some help with the dogs."

"Well, you were right," Po said. "They must really be a handful."

"It's tough enough to deal with all the regular care they need on an average day," Maggie said. "I can't imagine handling it when the family's under such stress."

"So, do you have someone who can help?" Po asked.

"Yes," Maggie said. "I had already talked to Catie about whether she'd be willing. She has always been good with Fitzgerald and the other dogs. She said she'd be happy to. And you know these kids. A little extra cash at that age is always a good thing."

"That's terrific," Po said. "What a perfect solution."

"There was one odd thing," Maggie said. "Melanie said Angela had proposed the same thing."

"Really?" Po said.

"I guess I shouldn't be surprised," Maggie said. "She worked for Mercedes as Fitz's handler for at least two years."

"It was nice of her to be thinking about what they'd need," Po said.

"You're right. She's very considerate," Maggie said.

"So, when does Catie start moonlighting?" Po asked.

"Today," Maggie said. "She's probably there now."

"Jack Francis and Jarrod have seemed so angry and suspicious," Po said. "It makes me feel better somehow that Melanie is willing to accept some help."

"I know what you mean," Maggie said. "I feel better, too."

"Did you get a chance to talk to Aaron?" Po asked.

"Yeah," Maggie said. "I think the food thing was just a misunderstanding."

"Really?" Po said.

"I think I hurt his feelings asking about it," Maggie said. "I'm sure it's just insult to injury, given everything else that's going on. But he said that Mrs. Spaeth had bought the food and then forgotten to take it with her on her way out. Julie asked if he'd mind dropping it off on his way home. He thought Angela knew about it, but Lynne was working the front desk, so she must not have."

"Poor kid," Po said. "But you had to ask."

"I know it," Maggie said. "But exactly."

"Could you do anything to reassure him?" Po asked.

"I did try," Maggie said. "Hopefully it will be OK. He's coming to work today. If we just do our regular thing, I think it will normalize."

After the friends hung up, Po thought about their conversation. "I'm taking Melanie's openness as a sign," she said to Hoover, who was lying on her feet, as usual. "Maybe the tide is turning."

CHAPTER 18

Slight, 18-year-old Catie Kilpatrick leaned back, stretching, and picked up the spray hose hanging on the wall. The tour and training were over, and it was time to wash down the runs for the seven dogs that lived in the glamorous kennel and shared a glamorous life with Mercedes Richardson. The first-class kennel, attached to the house. The high-end training area. The well-lit trophy case.

She walked down to the double-wide run on the end and greeted champion Fitzgerald. "Hi, baby," she said. "I'm sure you miss your mama."

"I wonder what will happen to them now," she thought.

While she liked Melanie and was happy to have the extra cash, she didn't think the young woman seemed like the serious dog type. And she'd seen plenty of it, working at the clinic, which catered to high-intensity dog owners.

"Nothing glamorous about this job. Poop scooper and kibble chef." Still, she liked it. "Here and Dr. Maggie's are about the only places you can play with sweet dogs and get paid," she thought, smiling. "It's worth the dirty work. And Dr. Maggie is a great boss. She always takes the time to explain things when I ask. And she trusts me."

Just the other day Maggie said how observant she was for noticing that T-Thomas—a normally ravenous-at-all-times basset hound, who tended toward the tubby side—had twice left half a meal untouched. Unheard of. "Maggie told everybody about that at the team meeting. And she seemed to think it was important when I told her what Mrs. Silversmith said. So I guess it was good that I brought it up. I wonder …"

Her thought was interrupted by a noise, like a cabinet shutting. But then she thought she must have imagined it, and she went back to her work. She didn't even bother to turn on her music when she was cleaning runs. The noise of the water drowned out everything else. "They are sure set up here," she thought. "Not many people would build a boarding facility onto their house."

She turned her attention to hosing down the first run. With the water turned on full force, she never heard the door open behind her. The blow that came was so hard, she never realized what had happened. She crumbled to the floor, dead.

CHAPTER 19

Po had her running shoes on and one foot out the door when her cell phone rang. She pulled off her gloves and pulled it out of her jacket pocket.

"Hello?" she answered, puzzled about who might be calling so early.

"Hi, Po," Maggie answered. "Did you see the news this morning?"

"No," she said. "Clearly I must have missed something important. What happened?"

"Oh, Po," she said, and there was a full minute of silence as Maggie clearly tried to control her voice on the other end.

"Someone killed Catie," she finally blurted out.

It didn't matter then that Maggie was incapable of talking, because Po was incapable of hearing. She shut the door and walked blankly to the closest chair, where she sat clutching the phone with her head between her knees willing herself to breathe.

"Po?" Maggie said finally. "Are you there?"

"Yes," Po managed. "I'm still here. How could this happen? What happened?"

"I don't know. I just can't believe it," Maggie said. "I feel terrible. I suggested her. I suggested the whole idea. And she was killed at the Richardsons'. Catie's parents... well can you imagine?!"

"Oh, my," Po said. She couldn't seem to get any further. Couldn't process the horror of this news. Couldn't even think about the sparkly young woman without her brain seeming to shut down.

"I have to go to the clinic today, Po," Maggie said with some desperation. "And our whole team will be feeling the way I do. I think I have to close for the day. That's the only thing I can do, I think. What do you think?"

"Oh, my," Po said again. "I hadn't thought that far yet. But you're probably right. I think that's the best approach."

"I'm sorry, Po," Maggie said. "I know that's the least of it. But I'm stretched so thin right now I can't think straight."

"No, you're entirely right," Po said. "And helping Catie's friends and co-workers through this is a big deal."

"OK," Maggie said. "I have to go think about what I'll

say and what we need to do to make that work. I'll call you back after."

Ten minutes later, Po was sitting in the same spot, staring at the wall. And her phone rang again. This time it was Kate.

"Po?" she heard her goddaughter say when she flipped the phone she was still holding back open.

"Hi, Kate," Po said. "I heard. Maggie just called."

"I can't believe it, Po," Kate said, a choked note in her voice. "I can't believe it."

"I've got to see the news," Po said. "Are you going to school?"

"Yes," Kate said. "I don't see how I can't."

"OK," Po said. "Let me see what I can learn. Call me when you get a chance."

And galvanized into action, Po walked into the den and flipped on the television, flipping between local channels until she caught the story that had spurred her early morning calls.

"The body of a young woman was found last night in the home of Mercedes Richardson," the announcer said solemnly. "Mrs. Richardson disappeared eight days ago. Police will comment only that the investigation of her disappearance is ongoing."

The image switched from the newscaster to a sequence shot in front of the Richardson house the night before, and the detective on the scene. "We cannot yet comment on this case," he said. "We are in the preliminary stages of evidence gathering and need to focus on that process with all the intensity we can bring to bear. Only then will we be able to start drawing conclusions about the motives in this homicide and any connection to the disappearance that is also under investigation."

The screen was filled once again by the news desk and the serious anchor.

"The name of the victim has not yet been released," he said.

Po's phone had buzzed again during the newscast, and she'd ignored it. Now she looked and saw that Eleanor had called. Not knowing yet what to say, she switched channels again, and caught the story again. Different anchor. Same limited set of facts. After one more round of channel-roulette she shut off the TV and sat in silence, trying to put together a cohesive thread of thought.

Eventually she stood back up and decided to go run. Sometimes that was therapeutic. So she put her gloves back on and headed out. Without any conscious thought about where she was headed, she found herself on one of her normal routes, headed down to Elderberry Road. She ran past Selma's store, The French Quarter, the Elderberry Bookstore, and Brew and Brie. And then by Flowers by Daisy, Marla's Bakery, and the antique store. But instead of seeing the familiar faces of the stores as she jogged past, she seemed to see various pieces of the puzzles from the past weeks. Aaron's face as he burst into the Queen Bees meeting just two Saturdays ago. Jarrod coming out of the coffee shop. Jack Francis' car parked down from the Ink Spot.

It seemed so much longer to Po. "So much has happened.

So difficult to understand violence. How could this happen in wonderful Crestwood? Who could have done these things? And why?"

As her feet pounded along her familiar morning path, her mind pounded down a similarly well-beaten trail, starting with Fitzgerald's disappearance. How could he have gotten out? Who would benefit by letting him out? Who could have had access to the clinic? Did the person mean for the champion dog to be found?

Asking herself the same questions yielded no more answers. Next she moved to Mercedes' disappearance. Is she really dead? Who could have hated her enough to kill her? Why had police not found her body?

"I have to be overlooking something," Po thought. "Something critical. The piece that makes this picture whole."

And now Catie.

Po thought about 18-year-old Catie. Her direct answers to Po's questions. Her cheerful thinking about caring for animals. Her poor parents, who would have to come to terms with this incredible loss.

And through it all, she kept putting one foot in front of the other. She kept thinking about how or who might connect these terrible events in her beloved town. And she kept struggling to believe it was all real.

The run helped get Po into her morning routine. She showered after, and dressed in a comfortable, soft turtleneck and a warm, quilted vest. Cocooning clothes, she thought as she put them on. She made coffee. She walked into her studio. And she ignored her phone, waiting for that somewhere-back-near-center feeling. It was a long time coming. "I'd settle for 'can see centered from here,'" Po thought as she tried to decide what to do. She needed to focus for a little while. Something that would keep her hands busy and her brain off the same "this just can't be" path she'd been running since she picked up the phone that morning.

She settled on preparing the binding for the Humane Society quilt. Repetitive; not too creative. That would do nicely, she decided. She started cutting long strips of the cloth the Bees had chosen, and she sewed them end to end. Then came the ironing. And she found the whole process soothing. The feel of the fabric under her fingers as she ran it through the sewing machine. The whirring of the needle as it flashed up and down. The bright color of the fabric and the warm iron. It gave her the moments of peace she needed. The next time the phone rang, she answered.

"I've been worried sick, Po," she heard Max say. "If you hadn't picked up, I was coming over to check on you."

"I'm sorry, Max," she said sincerely. "I just needed some quiet time. I was in the studio."

"So have you heard?" he asked.

"Yes," she said. "I've been so upset. Poor Catie."

"You need to be more careful," Max said.

"I'm careful," Po said, feeling a little stung.

"You think you are," Max said gently. "But this just proves how dangerous the current environment is. And you are mired in the very middle of the whole thing."

He paused. "I'm afraid for you, Po. And for Kate."

Po knew he had their best interests at heart, and for his sake, she took a deep breath and tried to step back.

"OK, Max," she said. "I will try. But I can't just abandon Maggie. She needs my help. And I can't stop watching over Kate. You know she'd keep looking for answers on her own."

"You could fall into a deep hole trying to help fix every problem that you think you could help with," Max said. " And you're too important to me to let that happen."

"OK," Po said again. "I will try."

But even as she hung up, she knew she couldn't just give up now. There were answers there, just beyond her reach. And she knew she could fix everything if she could just get to them. She would be careful. And she knew Max was right. But she couldn't give up. Not now.

Po was pondering her next step when she responded to a soft knock on her door and found a weary, pale looking Maggie standing on her doorstep.

"What a nice surprise," she said with a smile.

"I'm sorry to just drop by," Maggie said. "But I can't decide what to do."

"I'm having that problem," Po said.

"If I go home, I will just pull the covers over my head and try to sleep away this feeling," Maggie said, looking a little embarrassed. "And that's not going to help anybody. I was hoping I could come up with a plan if I came and talked with you about it."

"How'd it go this morning with your team?" Po asked as they walked to the kitchen. "That had to be so hard."

"It was pretty terrible," Maggie said. "But we managed. Everyone feels absolutely awful, of course. Angela and Lynne split up the calls and rescheduled everyone we'd have seen today. The rest of the crew took care of the animals that are at the clinic now. And then I sent everyone home."

"I'm sure they appreciate it," Po assured her.

"I figure they all need a chance to catch their breath, just the same as I do," Maggie said. "We have sure been through it, huh?"

"Yes, indeed," Po said with feeling.

"So, what can I do?" Maggie said. She smiled sadly. "I mean besides crawl back into bed for 24 hours."

"Let's strategize," Po said.

Together they outlined the possible suspects for each unexpected event. Fitzgerald's disappearance still had them somewhat stumped.

"Perhaps Jarrod was tired of investing in the dogs and their training," Maggie said. "That's pretty substantial. Or perhaps he wanted Mercedes to stop spending so much time on that hobby and more time with him."

"Could be," Po said, but she sounded unconvinced.

"Or maybe Jack Francis was trying to save Mercedes' money so she'd have more to help him out," Maggie tried again.

"Maybe," Po said.

"Or it could be anyone who knows anyone at my clinic and has a grudge," Maggie said, grumpily.

"Angela did leave on good terms, didn't she?" Po asked.

"Of course," Maggie said, surprised. "So good that she's still trying to help them out." She paused. "Not that you can tell with Mercedes. She's as cold toward Angela as she is toward anyone. Or she was."

"I'm just trying to make sure I don't overlook anything," Po said.

"You haven't asked me about Aaron," Maggie said.

"I just don't think it could be him," Po said.

"But why not?" Maggie said. "We have to question all our assumptions."

"OK, then," Po said. "What about Aaron? Could he have let Fitzgerald out on purpose? Or even by accident?"

"I guess I believe he might have let him out on accident," Maggie said slowly. "He sure wouldn't want to admit that after the confrontation with Mercedes. I'm not sure what he'd have been doing at the clinic, but there could be an innocent reason." She thought about it some more. "I guess I think that's possible."

"What about on purpose?" Po asked.

"I really don't think so," Maggie said. "I really do think he's a good kid. He's been very reliable. And diligent about trying to help during this terrible time. I just can't believe it."

Po sat thinking for a few minutes. And Maggie finally interrupted.

"We're really not getting anywhere here," Maggie said. "How about Mercedes?"

"Well, we have Jack Francis and Jarrod on the list again," Po said. "Jack Francis wants to inherit her money to bail out his dealership. Jarrod could be having an affair. Maybe he can't leave her without giving up his comfortable life."

"What about Aaron?" Maggie asked. "The police certainly think he's a suspect."

"He had a very public confrontation with Mercedes just a few days before she disappeared. She threatened his job and his future."

"But he would never!" Maggie interjected.

"I agree," Po said firmly. "But the police take that kind of thing pretty seriously. It's no surprise that he made the suspect list."

"OK," Maggie said. "But I still think it's impossible." She paused for a moment, and Po sunk back into deep thought.

"Besides," Maggie burst out again a minute later. "Do you know how many people have threatened to kill Mercedes in the last 10 years? I bet at least 50. She's unbearable!"

"I agree," Po said again. "We're just cataloging. Thinking. Doing the same thinking I've been doing every minute for hours, in fact. It doesn't seem to be helping. But I keep hoping we might figure out something new."

"I know it," Maggie said. "I'm sorry. I don't mean to be impatient. And none of this is your fault. You're the best for even talking it over with me. And you've done so much more. I'm just teetering over the edge."

Po smiled at her friend, and got up from her spot to walk around the coffee table and give her a hug. Then she resumed her spot and her thinking.

"I would bring up suspects for Catie, but I can't quite bear it," Maggie said quietly. Po just nodded.

"I tell you what," she said finally. "Jack Francis and Jarrod are on two lists each. Let's follow them."

"Really?" Maggie said, looking at her incredulously. "You mean it?"

"Yes," Po said. "Sitting around in front of Mercedes' house today has to be better than sitting around here, right?"

"Well… yes," Maggie said. "But it'll be a zoo, don't you think?"

"Probably," Po said. "But I don't have any other ideas. Do you?"

"No," Maggie admitted.

So they packed up a thermos full of coffee and a bag of biscotti, and they went on their first-ever stakeout.

CHAPTER 20

It turned out that Maggie was right—there was no way to get near the house. And they wouldn't learn anything that the three local TV stations didn't also pick up on and report at 5 o'clock.

"So we've got a choice," Po said. "Jarrod or Jack Francis?"

"I go with Jack Francis," Maggie said. "I know him better, since he's been coming into the clinic. And I don't like him that well."

And with that, Po headed for the dealership. There was a laundromat across the street, and she parked.

"Now what?" Maggie asked.

"I say we do some wash," Po said, and she dug the seat cover off the back seat, liberally covered with Hoover's hair, as always.

"You amaze me," Maggie said.

Five minutes later they had the seat cover in the washer, and they sat near the front window, looking at past issues of O, the Oprah magazine, and subtly keeping an eye on the comings and goings across the street. The seat cover was in the dryer and they were becoming bored an hour later. No sign of Jack Francis. Not that many visitors to the dealership. Just not much action.

"Any other ideas?" Maggie asked Po, eyebrows raised.

"We could lurk outside the club instead," Po said.

"It doesn't seem like we'd have any better odds there," Maggie said with a sigh.

"Here, have some more coffee," Po said, pouring from the thermos. She got up and put some more coins in the dryer, and then returned to her seat. Just in time, it turned out, to pick up her phone.

"Hi, Kate," she said.

"Where are you?" Kate asked. "I just swung by your house, but your car was gone."

"We're at the laundromat mat across the street from Jack Francis' dealership."

"A stakeout!" Kate said with enthusiasm. "I'll be right there."

"It bothers me a little that she's so excited," Po said to Maggie when she hung up. "Maybe this is a bad idea."

"I still think it's better than hibernating and hoping things get better," Maggie said.

"Maybe," Po said, and they both lapsed into silence, drinking from the ceramic mugs Po had brought along and waiting for their high-energy co-conspirator to put in her appearance.

They didn't have long to wait.

"Hi," Kate said with enthusiasm. "How long have you been here? What have you learned?"

"At least an hour, I'd say," Maggie responded. "And nothing."

"We did manage to wash my seat covers and drink some coffee," Po said with a smile.

"Hmm," Kate said. "Not exactly getting the gold medal in the spy business, are you two."

She plopped down in the chair next to Po and stared intently across the street.

"Did he even show up since you've been here?"

"Nope," Maggie said. "That would count as excitement in my book."

"How many customers, would you say," Kate asked, still focused on the lot across the street.

"A handful," Maggie said.

"Four," Po corrected. "And no buyers, if I'm any judge. They cruised by, smiled and nodded, but no real discussions. The sales guy's smile went away instantly when they left."

"Hmm." Kate said.

They sat for a couple more minutes, just watching her watch and think. And the wait was rewarded. Kate sat up abruptly, her eyes opened wide, and she turned to them, clearly excited.

"What?!" Maggie asked. "Nothing over there changed. I'm sure of it."

"But it did," Kate said with a smile. "Something changed since I was here."

"Oh, come on," Po said impatiently. "Out with it. What did we miss?"

"The last time I was here, I think the dealership was for sale," Kate said.

"Really?" Po said. "I don't remember that."

"I noticed it before, but I didn't think it was important," Kate said excitedly. "There was a banner in the window that said, 'Looking for an investment?' I remember because I was thinking about whether a classic car would be a decent investment or not. You know, cars are supposed to depreciate the second you drive them off the lot, and all. But maybe an antique car is different."

"Uh huh?" Maggie said.

"Well, now I'm thinking it meant investment like invest in this business. And now the sign is gone. Here, look." Kate dug deep in the backpack that lay at her feet and emerged victoriously with a small camera. She spent several seconds flipping from picture to picture until she found the one she was looking for. "See," she said passing it to Po. "Remember, I took this on the day that you showed me all the clinic photos?"

"Interesting," Po said.

"He doesn't seem to have any more business," Kate continued. "But he could have the prospect of a cash infusion."

"I'm buying that theory," Maggie said. "Are we about done here?"

"I am," Kate said. "I'm having dinner with P.J. tonight." She wrinkled her nose. "And he made me promise. No murder talk."

"Maybe that's better," Po said.

"I'm sure you're right," Kate agreed. "So, see you guys later. Excellent sleuthing!"

And she was off again.

"That girl just never slows down," Maggie said with exasperated admiration.

"I know," Po said. "I'm not sure I ever had her energy."

On the way back to Po's house, clean cushion covers back in place, they formed their next plan. They picked up the makings for dinner and vowed not to admit where they'd been when Max came by.

"He wouldn't understand," Po said, looking a little worriedly at her friend.

"I'm sure he wouldn't," Maggie said. "I went along, and I'm not sure I do."

CHAPTER 21

When Max arrived, Maggie and Po had the table set, a meat loaf in the oven, a salad on the table, and the wine poured.

"I am such a lucky man," he said beaming at the two of them.

"I'm glad you think so," Po said, throwing him a warm smile over one shoulder as she popped some green beans in the microwave. "I'm afraid Maggie and I are going to eat and run tonight. We want to meet the rest of the Bees at Selma's."

"Ah, right," Max said. "Queen Bees night."

While these Tuesday night get togethers were not official

meetings, Po almost always attended. So Max was used to this evening routine.

Many of the Elderberry shops stayed open on Tuesday nights. And Selma kept the store open until 9 p.m. She also made sure the back table was available for them, and really enjoyed these relaxed meetings.

It was a chance to chat and sew and relax. A rejuvenating time to escape into the joy of their textiles and threads with comrades who understood the endless appeal of every project.

True to their mission of relaxation and normalcy, Maggie and Po pulled out of the drive a few minutes after 7 and were ensconced in their favorite chairs at Selma's back table 10 minutes later. Selma had a reliable college student working for her, who was thrilled with the evening hours, so Selma and Susan both got to join them.

Phoebe typically missed on Tuesdays. Her boys' bedtime was an almost sacred ritual. So she was home tucking them in.

Eleanor was there. She'd brought a plate of lemon bars, one of her favorite cookies. "I'm always hoping that when I'm sour I can strike a balance with sweetness that's so good you guys will still gobble me up," she laughed any time she brought them. And it was true, the mix of sweet and tangy sour was practically irresistible.

"You sure never have to worry about taking home leftovers when you bring us these," laughed Susan.

There seemed to be an unspoken agreement among the friends not to discuss the traumatic events of the past couple of weeks. Instead they talked about the things they always talked about. Color and stitching. Projects and sketches for the ideas kicking around in their heads for down the road. The next exhibit that someone was thinking of pulling together. And they enjoyed each others' company tonight as much as ever.

Eleanor had brought her project, "'Endless Stripes' is the current working title," she joked. She was still arranging and rearranging her many strips of fabrics, and Po continued to love the results.

Po had taken a few of the leaves she was liking better, and she worked on making a couple more. She seemed to be happier with them the more small elements each leaf had. "They're just more interesting," she said, as she showed them to Eleanor.

She laughed. "You like to make it hard," she said. "But I certainly can't argue with your results. They look beautiful."

Kate had brought some striking fall-flavored squares she'd made at least a year ago. "Or embarrassingly, maybe it was two years," she said with a frown. She had pieced all the gold, rust, brown and burgundy fabrics into squares, but had never welded them into one piece.

"What have you been thinking about it that's holding you up?" asked Selma, who asked this question of fabric shoppers every day.

"It's just feeling wrong," Kate said. "If I could explain why, I'm sure I could fix it."

"Why don't you come with me, and we'll look at them with some different fabrics?" Susan suggested. "Maybe you need

Dog-Gone Murder

something with a little more contrast." And they wandered off to try some other combinations.

With Susan helping Kate, the quilting on their cat quilt for the benefit stopped, so Selma took a turn to keep the momentum going. Susan had been working hard on it, and had most of the cats quilted. Her work added a dimension that Po found thrilling. And it was more exciting for her, she thought, since she hadn't done the work herself.

When she'd come in, she'd looked closely at what Susan had done, and marveled at her finesse. "You always managed to do enough, but not too much," she said with a smile."

"I'm so glad you think so," Susan said. "I want it to be perfect, of course. And I feel like I've had to make a million decisions without you guys in the past two days. I'm totally relieved that you like it."

"I love it!" Po assured her. And the other Queen Bees reinforced her enthusiasm, leaving Susan feeling completely content with her contributions.

Maggie had brought a set of squares she'd bought at an antique store on her last lake vacation. "I had to," she said when she'd first shown them to the Queen Bees. "I just kept thinking about the woman who'd gotten so far on this project but not finished. I sure will need someone to finish the not-quite-done projects that I've got stuck in all my closets."

She got some, "oh my, me too" moans in response.

"If you're getting into that business, you could sure help me out," Kate told her.

"Well, we'll see. Maybe the impulse will pass," Maggie responded.

Tonight she was ironing the squares, which featured a large flower basket pattern. And Po had to admit, the bright colors—orange and gold and turquoise, mostly—were captivating.

"I bet those are from the late 1950s," she said, looking over at Maggie's work.

"They're not perfect," Maggie said. "Whoever did them had even more trouble than I do getting the corners to match. I think she was a little impatient. But somehow, I find that appealing."

"It's going to look great, Maggie," said Leah.

She was sitting quietly at the table knitting. "I know," she said when Maggie looked over at her knitting needles with her eyes raised. "Where's my project? But one of my friends at the college is about to get a new granddaughter. I have to focus or I won't be done in time."

And under her deft fingers, a small hat was forming into a darling strawberry. The ripe red berry was the bottom of the hat, with some green seed flecks. When she got the body of the hat deep enough, Leah would knit on some green leaves and a stem.

"I love your berry hats, Leah," said Kate, reappearing with Susan. "And the strawberry might be my favorite. Although I'll never forget the time you made the eggplant. That one was so cute."

"I still love the blueberries, too," Po said with a smile. Leah had knitted a blueberry for Po's last little granddaughter when she was born, and she looked darling in it. She had bright blue eyes that picked up the color. The pictures were still some of Po's favorites.

Dog-Gone Murder

Before the friends knew it, it was time to call it a night.

"I'll bring the quilt by tomorrow night so you can do the binding, Po," Susan said as Po and Maggie headed out. "That sounds perfect," Po said. "I'll be ready."

"That was great," Maggie said to her with a smile on the short drive back to Po's house, where she'd left her truck. "So fun. Totally normal."

"Yes, it was," Po agreed. "Perfect."

CHAPTER 22

In the next few days, Po couldn't help feeling there was something they were overlooking. She looked at all her pictures of the clinic again. She thought over everything they knew about Jarrod and Jack Francis and tried to figure out a next step that could prove one or the other of them guilty or innocent of dognapping or murder. She reviewed Maggie's visits again and listed the most commonly visiting clients in order. That list started with Mercedes. The top spending clients. Also topped by Mercedes. The client with the highest bill per visit. "Of course," Po said to Hoover, who was standing by for results. "Mercedes." But her lists didn't seem to get her any closer to any answers. They did seem to spell bad news for the future finances of Maggie's clinic if Mercedes and her dogs were really out of the picture. "Great," sighed Po after an hour at these exercises. "More bad news. That seems almost impossible."

She checked in with Maggie, who was struggling to get herself and her team back in a routine that seemed more normal and comfortable. "It could be better," Maggie said during one of their calls. "It's obviously going to take a while to get over a co-worker's murder. Some of our clients have called, and it's hard to know what to say to them. I've had a few ask questions when they've been in. If we suspect anyone. Who it could have been. Why anyone would do such a thing. The first time it happened, Lynne burst out crying."

"Oh, my," Po said in sympathy.

"Still, I guess it could be worse," Maggie said. "We haven't had a fire yet."

Po laughed. And gave thanks that Maggie could still make jokes, with all she was facing.

"How does Aaron seem to be doing?" she asked Maggie.

"He came to talk with me today," Maggie said. "He was questioned about Catie's murder, and I know that was upsetting him. But he had an ironclad alibi that day. He was at a full-day photography workshop for one of his classes. So I have to think that moves him down the list of suspects."

"Clearly the police think Catie's death is related to the other issues, then," Po said.

"Yes, I think so," Maggie said. "And I sure do, too. It just seems like too much coincidence. But I sure can't imagine what the link could be."

"Well, maybe Catie knew something about Fitzgerald's disappearance," Po speculated.

"You mean she was behind it?" Maggie asked.

"Not necessarily," Po said. "I mean, maybe. But maybe she just noticed something that could be incriminating to someone else."

"That's interesting," Maggie said. "Let me think about what she could have known. Maybe I'll look at all the work schedules for around that time and see if I see anything."

But the next time they talked, they hadn't come up with anything new.

"I'm tired of dead ends," Maggie said wearily.

When Po wasn't busy thinking and worrying, she was working on binding the quilt. Susan had dropped it off with the quilting done on Wednesday afternoon.

"Oh, Susan," Po said. "It looks wonderful. I love what you did…"

She smoothed her fingers over the swirls Susan had stitched into the border.

Susan smiled. "I'm so glad you like it," she said. "I was happy with it, too."

Po always thought the quilting added a lot to the piece. But this time, it seemed it gave the final quilt even more dimension than normal.

As she did the binding, she enjoyed the patterns of the stitching. Susan had used a variegated thread on the swirly border, and the change in color seemed to give it movement and energy.

They'd chosen a black-and-white check for the binding, one of Po's favorite fabric patterns. Something about it managed to seem modern and yet comfortable and classic. Po had a pile of coiled strips of fabric ready to go. And she'd sewn it on the otherwise finished quilt Wednesday evening. So over the next couple of days, she settled into her grandmama chair whenever she could to carefully stitch the folded edge of the binding to the back of the quilt, giving their special piece of jointly created art a self-contained frame. This stage was actually one of Po's favorites, giving her contemplative moments and a calm, repetitious job that left her in an almost meditative state.

When she started, she felt sort of antsy, full of bottled up energy. She wasn't even sure she could sit and do the necessary handwork. But when she started she found her typical calm eventually arrived. And while she didn't achieve a miraculous breakthrough in understanding that a calm mind sometimes brings, she did feel more centered.

"We'll get it figured out," Po thought to herself, during one stint in her grandmamma chair when she was stitching the binding. "I know we will. And everything will get back to normal."

On Friday night, she finished and pressed the binding, and she took the quilt to Adele's for the benefit the next night. The Queen Bees had decided to skip their normal morning meeting, for once, and make the benefit their official meeting. So Po just called Maggie and Susan to let them know the quilt was completely done and delivered. She knew they'd be thinking about it. The next day, she thought, they could celebrate another achievement together.

"Too bad we'll still have so much of this dark cloud hanging over us," Po thought as she finally drifted off to sleep.

CHAPTER 23

Po wouldn't have to wait forever for the other shoe to drop, of course. On Saturday morning, Po's phone rang at 10. "Can I come over, Po?" she heard Kate say.

"Of course, Kate. Is everything alright?" The horrors of the past few days made her say this. And she sat with her heart in her throat as she waited for the answer.

"Uh huh, everything's fine," she said. "I just need to talk to you."

"OK," Po said. "In that case, I can't wait."

"I'll be there in five minutes," Kate said. And she was true to her word.

She pulled up in the driveway on her bike, hair flying, and propped her preferred vehicle by the front door, as she'd done since she was old enough to ride. Then she knocked gently before she let herself in.

"I couldn't stand it," she said, giving her godmother a hug. "I had to come tell you in person."

"Tell me what," Po asked, holding her back to look at her.

"They arrested Jack Francis this morning for Catie's murder," Kate said. "P.J. called to tell me." She shrugged and gave Po a small smile. "I've been asking him about it fairly frequently."

Po laughed. "I'm sure you have," she said. She remembered Kate's stubborn streak as a 4-year-old, and as a 14-year-old. She didn't think much had probably changed. In other words, the slim young woman standing before her was a force of formidable tenacity.

"Well, P.J. said I could know as much as they'd tell the reporter," Kate said. "She's been hounding him for information, too, so at least I'm not the only one."

"What else did he tell you?" Po asked.

"Here's the bare bones," Kate said. "They found the murder weapon. A tire iron. She was bludgeoned on the back of the head."

"How awful," Po said quietly.

"They found her in the kennel, but the water was turned off. It looks as though she was cleaning the cages when he attacked her. They also found a big stash of cash hidden in the Jack Francis' wing of the house. That's not necessarily a crime, of course, but it doesn't look good when he's been talking so publicly about being strapped."

"But why would he kill Catie?" Po asked.

"That part is not entirely clear," Kate said. "Either the police don't know, or they're not releasing what they suspect, since P.J. won't say. But I think it looks like she must have known something that implicates him in Mercedes' disappearance, don't you?"

"It does look that way," Po agreed.

"He was supposed to be at work at the time, but wasn't," Kate said.

"Do you think this means Aaron is off the suspect list?" Po asked.

"It seems like he should be," Kate said.

"That's good news at least," Po said, "although I feel a little bad thinking any of this is good news. But still."

"I know it," Kate said. "It's all so terrible. But imagine the injustice of arresting that boy if he hasn't done anything."

"It's an ill wind that blows nobody good," Po quoted. "I guess I'll just start hoping that the good here is for Aaron," Po said.

"I'll pick up the afternoon paper," Kate said. "Then we can see what spin the reporter puts on it."

"Sounds good," Po said. "Should I buy my own, or will you bring it by?"

They agreed that Kate would stop back by later. And with that, Po sighed, feeling some of the week's unbearable tension release. Maybe they were finding their way to the end of this nightmare.

That afternoon Kate came by as promised. "Here it is," she said, flourishing a newspaper as she walked through the front door. "I picked it up at the corner."

"Hey, now," Po said, as Hoover practically tripped her in his excitement to peer out the front door as she went to close it. "You go out back and give me a minute of peace."

Then she put on a kettle to boil as Kate sat down to read the article. When she finished, Kate pushed her unruly mass of curls over one shoulder, her classic gesture of impatience, and handed Po the article.

"What do you think?" Po asked, looking up when she'd finished and putting her reading glasses down on the solid coffee table.

"I can't decide whether to be frustrated or happy," Kate said, jumping up to tend to the kettle, which started whistling. "I was hoping to learn something. Get a spark. You know," she said. "On the other hand, it looks like P.J. told me absolutely everything he could." She smiled at Po. "He gets points for that, you know."

"I really do adore that young man, Kate."

"I know you do. And you are easily distracted by the matter of my heart," she said with a smile. "It seems like we have bigger fish to fry today."

"You're right, of course," Po said with a smile. "Back to fish."

About two sips into her cup of tea, Po realized Hoover hadn't come back to the door.

"I wonder where he is," she said to Kate. "He isn't usually that interested in hanging outside if there's company in here."

"I'll go take a look," Kate said. "After all, I know the corners of your yard intimately." Which she did. She'd logged as many hours outside on tag as she had inside on hide and seek.

She grabbed a jacket and went out as Po watched. Her first step was to check the gate. Hoover didn't have any qualms about taking advantage of the meter reader's lack of caution if it meant he could explore the neighborhood at will. But no, he should still be inside.

Shrugging at Po with a smile, Kate called to him, and then headed to his most likely refuge, a row of ancient forsythia bushes growing near the back fence. The bushes were almost 6 feet tall, and the slender branches almost touched the ground, forming a round cave of sorts with a cluster of tough stems near the center.

Seconds later Kate came running back around the edge of the green barricade.

"Po, call Maggie. There's something wrong!"

Suddenly hot and cold with fear, Po dialed the clinic number. As it rang, she ran down to the spot where Kate had disappeared. By the time Angela answered, she was kneeling next to Hoover. He was trying to get to his feet, but when he managed it, he seemed to stumble and lose his balance. There was clearly something wrong with him.

Po was just processing these symptoms when Angela answered the phone.

"Oh, Angela," Po knew the anxiety permeated her voice. "There's something wrong with Hoover!"

"Bring him in right away," Angela said when Po described his behavior. "We're officially closed, but I know Dr. Maggie will want to see Hoover herself. I'll give her a call to let her know that you're coming in, and I'll be watching for you."

Between them, Kate and Po managed to get a clearly distressed Hoover into Po's car. They drove to the clinic as quickly as they could, and Angela came running out when they pulled up to help them into the practice. Maggie arrived when they were at the door, maneuvering Hoover onto a rolling treatment table. Maggie gave Po a small smile and wheeled the agitated dog back to the treatment area.

In a few minutes she came back and led Po to her office.

"What's wrong with him?" Po asked, with worry thick in her voice and her insides tight with anxiety.

"He's showing the symptoms of ingesting antifreeze," Maggie said. "Did you see him getting into anything?"

"No," Po said. "And he wasn't out of the yard, or anything." She turned to Kate. "You didn't see him with anything, did you?"

"No, but I wasn't looking for that, I guess," she said.

"Well," Maggie said. "That's sure what it looks like. And the key is to keep him from metabolizing it, so it doesn't hurt his kidneys."

"I see," said Po, feeling a little dazed.

"The first thing we did was give him something to make him vomit," Maggie said. "And now we're going to wash out his stomach. Then I'll give him activated charcoal, which will bind with any of the poison that's left."

"OK," Po said, with a small nod to indicate her understanding.

"We're also giving Hoover intravenous fluids, to help wash

out his kidneys," Maggie said. She looked closely at Po and put her hand on her shoulder. "I think he's going to be fine, Po."

Po's eyes filled suddenly, and she nodded. "Thank you for helping him, Maggie," she said. "You're the best."

"We were lucky," Maggie said. "I might not have guessed so quickly that that's what was wrong with him except we saw a similar case just a couple of weeks ago."

"I do still want to keep him overnight," Maggie said, "so we can keep him on the fluids and keep an eye on him."

"OK," Po said.

"It's going to take us a little while to finish up with him," Maggie said. "You could wait here, if you want. Or you could come back in an hour or so and check on him if you wanted."

"I think I'd like to just wait, if that's OK," Po said.

"Of course," Maggie said. "I'll come out and get you when we're done." And she disappeared to take care of Hoover. Kate and Po settled into the chairs in Maggie's office, and Po tried to read one of the magazines in the stack on the side table.

"He'll be OK," Kate said gently when she looked over to see Po staring into space.

"I know," Po said. "Maggie is terrific, and she'll do everything she can for him. But I can't help feeling upset." She smiled wanly at Kate. "This is my first emergency visit in years."

"Luckily that Angela knew where to find Maggie," Kate said.

"That's for sure," Po said. "This day seems so out-of-whack.

Normally we'd all have gone to our Bees meeting this morning. And then I often run some errands. I might not have found him in time."

The two lapsed into silence as they waited. And it was with relief that they saw the smile on Maggie's face when she came back an hour or so later.

"I really think he's going to be fine," Maggie said, giving Po a hug.

"Oh, I'm so relieved," Po said, and she couldn't have meant it more.

"I've still got him on fluids," Maggie said. "And we'll keep a close eye on him, of course."

"Thank you so much," Po said. "Can I go back and see him?"

"Sure," Maggie said.

So Po and Kate went back and petted and cooed at Hoover, who really did look remarkably better than he had. "Thank goodness for Maggie," Po said.

"No doubt," agreed Kate.

Po didn't want to tie up Maggie's whole afternoon, so before too long she took her leave of Hoover and went to the front desk to pay her emergency bill.

"I know the clinic is closed tomorrow," Po said. "But do you think there's any way I could pick Hoover up? I sure hate to have him gone an extra night. Unless he needs additional care, of course."

Angela smiled. "I know Dr. Maggie will want to see him in the morning. So maybe we can arrange something. I'll talk to her about it and see what we can arrange."

"I'll stick around at home," Po said. "So you'll be able to reach me anytime."

Kate looked at her with surprise. "But the fundraiser is tonight," she said. "You're not going to miss that, are you? Dr. Maggie's been talking about it all week."

"Well, I may need to," Po said gently.

"Nonsense," Angela said. "I know from Dr. Maggie how hard you've all been working on the quilt for that. I'll be able to call in plenty of time before to let you know when you can pick Hoover up."

"But what if something happens later?" Po protested.

"We have your cell phone right here in the file," Angela assured her. "He will be fine, right here getting the care he needs. And if anything at all happens, I promise to call you."

"You really can't miss this, Po," Kate pleaded. "It just wouldn't be the same without you."

"What time does it start?" Angela asked.

"At 7:30," Po said.

Angela made a note in the file next to her number.

"It will all be fine," she said. "Go and have a wonderful time."

So, in the end Po conceded. Angela called later to say that Maggie would meet Po in the morning at 10 a.m. so she could pick up Hoover, assuming he continued to recover overnight. And so Po called Max to tell him about her traumatic day and to arrange her plans for the evening.

"I know you've been planning this for ages," he said apologetically. "But I've bumped into a problem. I think I'm going to need to meet you there."

"That's fine," Po said. "I'll be watching for you."

"I can't wait," Max said.

And Po decided everyone was right. It was best to go to the fundraiser and enjoy it, rather than sitting around and worrying. So she went and got ready. She picked out a deep amber-colored, feminine flared skirt and a tailored boiled wool jacket that set it off perfectly, a gift from her daughter. "It's amazing how the people who know you best can pick something like this that's just right," Po thought as she put it on.

And then with a glance at the empty dog bed where Hoover would normally be settling down to await her return, Po headed out.

CHAPTER 24

The fundraiser for the animal rescue league was being held at Adele Hartwick's B&B, as she had promised almost a year before. They had decorated the house for fall, and it looked much as it had at the open house a year ago, with dozens of pots of mums in rusts and gold in the warm entryway. Po walked up the majestic staircase, sinking into the thick green carpet that lined the stairs, and ropes of garlands lit with tiny white lights were wound around the walnut railing. A harvest tree stood sentinel at the landing, decked out with gold and silver pinecones, some real, some antique glass ornaments. In a prominent spot against the back wall hung the quilts the queen Bees had made for Adele, in tribute to her brother Ollie, an amateur astronomer. It was a brilliant galaxy, a swirl of golden and white star like strips, mixed into a background of midnight blue blocks. Po smiled, enjoying the final product of their combined effort in its place of honor.

"Come on down, Po," Adele called from the wide doorway to the dining room.

Po obliged, and was joined in less than a minute by Eleanor, who'd just arrived. They were both quickly provided with a glass of chardonnay and an outline of the events to come.

"This way," called Adele over her shoulder.

"Wow," Po said softly.

"You outdid yourself, Adele," Eleanor concurred.

Adele looked pleased. In fact, Po thought, she'd really never seen her look so happy. The first year of running a bed and breakfast had agreed with her.

"Well, I wanted it to be perfect for you," she said.

They had moved the chairs out and carefully laid the table with the items that were available through the silent auction. And she'd hung the quilt the Bees had made behind the table, where it could be seen easily from every corner of the room.

She smiled at their reactions. "I know how wonderful your work is, of course," she said.

Besides the galaxy quilt in the hall, the Queen Bees had made eight quilts for the bed and breakfast—a job Adele had commissioned—each one different. And this unique touch was one that guests rarely failed to mention to their hostess.

Po moved closer to the table, to take a look at the many other items available for bidding. There were bidding forms and pens set out conveniently. And the array of items was impressive. Of course, there were many pet-themed options. Two giant gift baskets with gourmet treats from Three Dog Bakery caught her eye. Hoover was particularly fond of the drooly dream bars, peanut flavored bars with carob chips—a doggie confection that just couldn't be beat. And he wouldn't say no to a beagle bagel, she was certain.

There was a similar cat treat basket with toy mice; catnip balls; a feather laced delicately to the end of a stick, for playful pouncing; and more, donated by one of the pet supply stores in town. The travel agency had arranged a cruise, and also a package for six to spend a week in the south of France.

Po put in a bid on one of the treat baskets for Hoover, making a mental note to try not to overindulge him if she won it. She had been neglecting his walks, and really he could use extra exercises not less. But it would be hard. She had a strong urge to give him anything his little heart desired after what happened today.

"They're going to rake in the cash, huh, Po?" came a voice from her right, interrupting her reverie about pet fitness. She turned to see platinum haired Phoebe, her halo of hair glistening and her petite figure wound in a sari-inspired wrap of silvery gold that made her look like a fun-loving angel.

"I sure hope so," Po said with a smile. She stepped back from the table to admire Phoebe, decked out in evening finery. "You look just stunning."

Phoebe leaned in closer. "I wanted to attach a tail to the back, in the spirit of celebrating pets, but Jimmy said it just really wouldn't be appropriate." She laughed, a pealing laugh that was full of fun, and seemed to bounce around the room. That was enough to make her husband turn around and smile, and in moments he was by her side, as tall and dark as she was petite and blond.

Within 20 minutes, the bed and breakfast was bustling with guests for the event, and a subset of the Queen Bees found themselves in a corner. "A toast," Po said, raising her glass. "To friendship."

"To friendship," the group echoed, and more than one eye among them was clouded with a tear as they thought about the challenges of the last week.

"I don't know what I would every do without all of you," Po said sincerely.

"You'd have to find some other crazy friends to quilt on a deadline," Phoebe laughed. And they turned to look at the playful quilt hanging over the table.

"I peeked, and there seem to be a few bids already in the canister next to the quilt," Kate said. "Hopefully our creation will really help."

"Food and cozy lodgings for the stray dogs and cats of the world," Eleanor said. She tossed the end of her perfectly coordinated raw silk scarf back over her right shoulder. "Hopefully Maggie will be here soon to enjoy what will doubtless be a wonderfully successful evening. I'm a little surprised she's late."

"She must have had an emergency," Phoebe said knowingly. Just then, Po felt her phone start to vibrate inside her evening bag. That was an upside to leaving her various totes and backpacks at home in favor of a clutch—in this case one crusted in mother-of-pearl buttons. She could only fit a few things in, so it was clear when one was buzzing. She hurried off to a slightly quieter corner, her heart in her throat as she recognized the number from Maggie's clinic.

"Hello?" she said.

"Hi, Mrs. Paltrow," she heard Angela answer. "I know you're at the Humane Society event, but I was sure you'd want me to call. I'm concerned about Hoover."

"What's wrong?" Po asked, worry filling every bit of her mind and an instant knot of tension forming in her stomach. "I thought he was out of the woods."

"I think you'd better come in," Angela said.

"I'll be right there," Po assured her. And as soon as she'd hung up, she started working her way toward the entrance. The Bees were still busy talking over by the donations table. She collected her coat and headed out. On the way to the clinic she called and left Max a message letting him know where she'd gone. "I don't want him showing up to find me missing and worry," she thought. "He's probably on his way now."

And that was her last thought except of worry about her four-legged companion.

CHAPTER 25

Po parked behind the building and let herself into the side door of the clinic, which was open, as Angela had promised. She rushed around the corner to the treatment area, and found Hoover in a run, looking just as he had when she left. Sleepy, but with a slow wag for her when she peered in at him.

"I think he's going to be OK after all," Angela said. "But I'm not so sure about you."

Po stood up, and as she did some of the pieces of the puzzle that she'd been struggling with slid suddenly into place.

"You just had to keep digging, didn't you," Angela said. "You couldn't just let well enough alone.

Angela kept moving toward her, and suddenly Po noticed the gun in her hand. In that moment, her brain seemed to be running on superspeed, and yet everything else seemed to be moving very slowly, like the whole world was stuck in molasses.

"What happened, Angela?" she asked. "Why are you doing this?"

If she could just keep her busy for a minute or two, Po thought. Angela shook her head. Po kept cataloging the contents of the room. Maybe there was a way out of this. Just keep talking, she thought.

"You care so much for people. I don't understand," Po said, her eyes returning to Angela.

Angela took a deep wavering breath.

"How could you understand?" she said. "You have everything. That's how it always is. I never get a break. The people with all the breaks never notice."

"You've been so successful here, though," Po said. "I thought you were happy."

"I have practice putting a good face on things," Angela said. "I deserve more."

Po's mind was still scrambling. Looking for a way out of this trap. Hoping Maggie didn't arrive too soon. With bad timing they could both wind up facing the wrong end of the gun. Or maybe she should be hoping Maggie did arrive soon. Maybe she could figure out a better plan than hers: stall and hope to not get shot.

"Did you shoot Mercedes?" she asked, gesturing to the gun.

"Oh, come on," Angela said with a sneer that looked foreign to Po on her normally pleasant face. "Didn't you figure it out? You have all the pieces; I'm sure of it."

She kept the weapon trained on Po as she moved toward the drug safe. "Come on," she taunted. "What've you got? I know you can put the pieces together. That's why you're here, after all."

"Because you thought I knew it was you?" Po asked.

"Because I know you'd put it together eventually," Angela clarified. She smiled grimly. "Lucky for me you didn't get there before I'd put together a plan to get rid of you."

"So, you let Fitzgerald out? To get Aaron in trouble?"

"No," Angela said dismissively. "He's not worth my time. I did it to get some leverage on Mercedes. And to keep her focused on someone besides me, if I decided I didn't need the leverage." She paused. "I have to admit, that didn't work out the way I'd planned."

Angela leaned against the counter, the gun still trained on Po. From Po's point of view, that was somehow an improvement. She seemed to be distracting Angela from the task at hand, which seemed to be killing her.

"I thought I heard you arguing with someone on the phone one day when I was here," Po said. "Who was that?"

"You noticed that, did you," Angela snarled. "See, you do have the pieces. That was Jack Francis. He wanted me to kill Fitz. But he's just too special. There's not another dog like him. Not anywhere."

"Why would he want Fitzgerald killed?" Po asked.

"He hoped that Mercedes would be so heartbroken she'd quit showing dogs," Angela said. She sniffed. "Shows what he knows. Mercedes would never have stopped. She'd find a new champion and spend all her money on the new dog instead. I bet it wouldn't have taken her a month to move on."

"Why did you ever stop working with him?" Po asked. "You seem to care about him so much. You must have loved being his handler."

"I was the best," Angela said. "And she replaced me in two weeks. That's how she is."

"But why?" Po asked.

"She didn't appreciate me. She didn't care that she didn't pay me enough to live on. She didn't care that she had me working every weekend. She didn't see that Fitz would never have been the dog he is without me."

Angela's face hardened even more. "She didn't deserve him."

"But you helped Aaron find Fitzgerald, didn't you. So you helped Mercedes get him back. After you helped Jack Francis by letting him out."

"Now you've got it," Angela said.

"But why?"

"I told you—she didn't deserve him."

"I don't understand," Po said.

"She just cared about Fitz as property. How much recognition he could earn for her. How much prize money he could earn. How much his pups would sell for. She didn't care about him. Even when I took him, all she cared about was the money."

Angela took a shaky breath.

"She didn't deserve to get him back. But that was the only

way to get her here. And I knew I needed to set Fitzgerald free for real."

"You killed her, didn't you."

"Finally got there, didn't you," Angela said. "Of course I did. And Fitzgerald was the motivation and the bait. With Mercedes gone, I will be able to talk those selfish kids of hers into giving him up, no problem. They don't want to spend the money or do the work. They'll be happy to see him go. They'll sell him to me for a reasonable price, and I can go back to showing him."

"But Mercedes wouldn't let him go."

"Of course not," Angela scoffed. "Grabby witch. She couldn't stand that he responded better to me than he did to her. She would never have let me have him. She'd keep me away just to spite me."

"So you killed her."

"Right here," Angela said. "Just like I'm going to kill you."

And with that, she seemed to refocus. Still keeping an eye on Po, she typed a password into the keypad on the drug safe, and she drew out a vial.

"What are you doing?" Po asked, feeling shaky and trying not to show it.

"You'll just feel one sharp prick," Angela said with a twisted travesty of her old smile.

"You killed Mercedes here?" Po asked, trying desperately to distract Angela again. "They found the car near Aaron's house."

"Because that's where I left it," Angela said. "I need to think about where to leave yours. But there's time for that."

Dog-Gone Murder

She started advancing toward Po, armed now with the gun and a loaded syringe.

"What's that?" asked Po, nodding to Angela's left hand, the one with the long needle. It was tough to decide which seemed worse, getting shot, or getting injected with a mysterious, likely deadly chemical. Getting shot was actually beginning to win out in her mind. "Quicker, probably, and harder to cover up," she thought, with the small part of her brain that was still capable of analyzing the situation and looking for options. Instinctively, she'd been backing away from Angela's slow and wary approach.

"Stop moving!" Angela snapped. "Or I'll shoot you right now. Don't think I won't."

Po knew she'd misjudged as soon as she moved, but couldn't correct. Angela had anticipated her lunge toward the door, and Po felt the needle she'd been wielding penetrate her skin and deep into her muscle. And then less than a second later she felt the sting as Angela depressed the plunger.

Within seconds she started to feel a deep sense of relaxation flood through her body. An odd sense of well-being, even. Her anxiety faded and she felt an odd urge to laugh, though she wasn't sure about what.

Vaguely she was aware of Angela standing a few feet away, watching. Although she seemed to be having trouble keeping her in focus.

"There, then," she heard Angela say, as if through a fog. "See, that wasn't so bad."

"Stop! Stop! Fight!" cried half of Po's brain from a distance. But she couldn't seem to harness the thought. "I bet this is how Mercedes felt," she thought vaguely. "I am going to die." And yet she didn't really feel any anxiety. She felt another prick and a dark cloud seemed to fall. A sharp bark from Hoover was the last thing she heard.

CHAPTER 26

When Po opened her eyes, she found herself in a sterile hospital bed, wearing a gown and hooked to an IV with no idea how she'd gotten there. Just as she was getting her thoughts together to wonder, Kate came in.

"You're awake!" she whispered excitedly.

"What happened?" Po asked. "I thought it was all over."

"You lucked out," Kate said. "Thank goodness. We could have lost you." Her eyes filled and she fell silent for a moment.

Po patted her hand. "Come on," she said. "It's all OK now. Tell me what happened."

"OK," Kate said, getting control of herself. "Here's the part I know."

She took a breath.

"When Maggie arrived at the party, she asked where you were. We thought you were just in another room, but when we did a sweep, we didn't find you. We called your cell phone, but you didn't answer. So Maggie called Max."

"That was smart," Po said. "It's sure a good thing I have you guys to check up on me."

"No doubt," Kate said dryly. "So, Max told us you'd gone to meet Maggie at the clinic, because there was something wrong with Hoover. But Maggie was with us. Angela had called her, but about another patient. That's why she was late to the benefit. But she hadn't said anything about Hoover."

"Angela knew all about our plans for tonight," Po said. "We'd talked about it earlier. She and Maggie convinced me to go to the benefit. Then she delayed Maggie. That made her story to me plausible." She paused.

"Hoover's all right, isn't he?" Po asked next.

"Yes," Kate said. "He was fine all along. Maggie thinks she gave him a sedative, so he would look a little droopy when you got there, but she said that won't hurt him. And he seems to be recovering fine from the antifreeze poisoning."

"That was Angela, too, wasn't it," Po said.

"Probably," Kate agreed. "I don't think we know how she managed it, yet. But it does seem too convenient to be coincidence."

"So, you figured out I'd gone to the clinic, and that it was probably a set up, since Angela didn't tell Maggie about it. What then?"

"Well," Kate said. "I called P.J. He started for the clinic and called in for back up."

"I'm sure he told you to stay where you were, too. Right?" Po said.

"Uh huh," Kate said.

"And you ignored him?" Po guessed.

"Maggie and I called Max back and headed for the clinic ourselves," Kate confirmed.

Po smiled. "You are my darling girl," she said. "But you know that's the last thing I would have wanted. I promised your mom that I'd look after you."

"I know," Kate said. "But I couldn't have lived with myself if you'd died and I hadn't gone to try to help." Her face crumpled a little. "I just couldn't."

She leaned in for a hug, and Po stroked her hair. "I know you couldn't," she said soothingly. "And it's all OK. We're all safe, and that's what matters."

"Max ran over to check on Maggie," Kate said when she finally emerged from the hug. "But I promised to call him when you woke up. The doctors weren't sure how long it would take for the drugs to wear off."

"Is Maggie OK?" Po asked, suddenly worried.

"Yes," she's fine," Kate assured her. "We really weren't in any danger. The police pulled up at the same time we did, and they surrounded the building. Maggie opened the door, and they sneaked in. They were just in time to save you, and Angela was so focused on you, she didn't even see them coming."

"It had to be traumatic to be outside the building with all that happening inside," Po said.

"We were sick with worry," Kate agreed. "It was terrible to wait. And then the ambulance came and they brought you out. I was so scared."

"Thanks to all of you I seem to be fine," Po said.

"It all seems so surreal," Kate said. "I just would never have believed it was possible."

"That what was possible?" Po asked.

"Well, I guess I believed everything you and Maggie said about Angela. And she certainly seemed completely nice when we took Hoover in. But look what she was capable of." Kate took Po's hand again.

"It is shocking, I think, any time you bump into someone who's really capable of hurting others," Po said thoughtfully. "I feel like we can be kind of callous. You hear about people dying violent deaths all the time on the news and on TV. But when it happens to someone you know…" She trailed off.

"OK," Kate said with a little shake of her head. "I promised Max." She dialed the phone and handed it to Po.

The next day Po's doctor released her, and Max and Kate brought her some clothes to wear home and picked her up. They watched her carefully on every step up the walk and opened the door for her.

"I really am OK, you two," she said finally, as they settled her in her favorite chair and started working on a fire and a cup of tea.

"I know you are," Max said with a warm smile as he piled kindling. And then he stopped, sat down on the arm of the chair and took her hand. His eyes seemed to cloud over. "But when I think..."

Po squeezed his hand back. "But there aren't any might-have-happeneds," she said.

"True," Max acknowledged. "But we were lucky."

He went back to fire building. "I don't supposed I can convince you to start locking your door, can I?" he asked, looking over his shoulder at her as he reached for the long fireplace matches she always kept near at hand.

"No," she smiled.

"Maybe you are all right, then," he said.

Kate had been clattering in the kitchen, and when she walked over, she was carrying a plate of biscotti and a pot of tea.

"Sustenance," she said with a flourish as she lay them down.

"That looks terrific," Po said, pouring some into her favorite teacup, which was bedecked with thistles. "Now, tell me what you've learned since yesterday. And what you left out, because you were worrying about my state of health and didn't want me overly excited."

Max and Kate looked at each other over her head, but Po intercepted the glance.

"See," she said. "I knew it was true. You've been with-holding."

Max gave Kate a small nod, took a seat in the corner of the sofa nearest Po, and claimed his own cup of tea.

Kate settled on the stone ledge that extended in front of the fire, her favorite perch since she was a young girl, and thought for a moment before she started.

"It turns out, Angela was setting people up all over," Kate said. "So you were right, Po. All the trouble was connected, and she was at the center. She was really a master of deception. And the misleading phone call seemed to be her specialty."

"What do you mean," Po asked.

"Take, for instance, the day Aaron found Fitzgerald," Kate said. "Remember, she called Mercedes to say that Aaron would be bringing him by."

"Right," Po said.

"Well, what actually happened was that she called Mercedes and told her to come pick Fitzgerald up. She knew from talking to Jack Francis that Jarrod was going fishing and that he and Melanie were going to meet some friends. So, she arranged for Aaron to be at the house when there were no witnesses. And at the same time, she lured Mercedes to the clinic at a time when she knew it would be deserted, too."

A disbelieving Po could only shake her head.

"And there's more," Kate said. "After she'd talked to Mercedes on her cell phone, she called the main number at the house and left a message saying that Aaron would come by."

"Did you hear all this from P.J.?" Po asked.

"Yeah," Kate said.

"Surely this means Aaron is completely cleared of any

suspicion, then," Po said.

"I sure think so," Kate said. "He actually went by to talk to Maggie about it. I think he just needed to hear someone else say it was over. She said he seemed relieved, and yet upset, somehow."

"Just imagine the trauma that boy's been through," Max interjected. "And pretty much on his own, too. I wouldn't be surprised if it took him a while to get over it."

"Then she pulled a similar phone trick with Maggie and me," Po said.

"Well, it worked before, didn't it?" Kate said.

"You know," Po said, "I really wasn't nearly as close to the answer as Angela thought. I was just asking a few of the right questions."

"But to a guilty conscience, every time you asked another question it must have seemed that you knew," Kate said.

"What about Catie?" Po asked hesitantly. "What put her in Angela's path?

"I think it was the same thing as with you," Kate said. "I'm not sure we have all the answers, but it sounds like she thought she knew more than she did."

"Do you have any idea what?" Po asked.

"Maggie will know more," Kate said. "But it sounds like Catie might have noticed a discrepancy in the drug log. If she'd mentioned that to Angela either before or after she brought it up with Maggie, that might have been enough."

"So Angela suggested to Maggie that Catie could help out the Richardsons in their time of need. And probably told Catie how great it would be and offered advice."

"Right," Kate said. "And she offered to rearrange her work schedule if need be. So she knew exactly when Catie would be there."

"And she killed her," Po said softly.

They all fell silent for a moment thinking again about the enthusiastic young woman.

"Angela tried to frame Jack Francis for the murder," Kate went on finally. "She sure had me believing."

"I think Jack Francis had become a problem for her," Max said. "He may have been a co-conspirator in the disappearance of Fitzgerald. And he and Jarrod both knew that Mercedes had fired Angela because she suspected her of petty theft. So when Mercedes disappeared, he probably threatened to turn her in."

"On the flip side," Kate took up the story, "he had a terrific motive for killing Mercedes himself. Angela probably had some evidence that he was involved in the dognapping, and he didn't have an alibi. That seems to have been keeping him in check. But getting him convicted for murder clearly would be a more secure situation."

"Clearly," Po said, a bit dryly.

"I don't have the evidence for this yet," Max said, "but I'm willing to bet that Angela was stealing from Maggie's practice, too. That could easily explain her financial problems. She was trying to implicate Aaron, and given all her other misdirection…. Well, you see what I'm saying."

"Poor Maggie," Po said. "How's she holding up?"

"She seems to be managing," Kate said. "But she's been better for sure."

"We actually suggested to her that she come by and check on you this afternoon," Max said. "I think it will make her feel better to talk with you. And it will get her out of the house."

"That will be wonderful," Po said.

"I think it's going to be awhile before she feels like everything is back to normal at the clinic," Kate said, with a hint of her former worry for her friend.

"I'm sure you're right, Kate," Po said. "But hopefully we'll be able to help."

Max raised his eyebrows. "'Helping' does not in this case include stakeouts, I trust," he said.

"No," Po promised. "No more stakeouts. I've had my fill of dangerous pastimes and learned my lesson."

"OK, then," Max said. "If you're sure of that, I guess I can leave you two unsupervised, at least for a couple of hours while I run some errands."

"We'll be fine," Po said. "I promise."

"Me, too," Kate chimed in. "I promise."

And they were true to their word. They drank the tea and talked. Made another pot and a batch of shortbread, and talked over everything with Maggie when she arrived. And when Max and P.J. found their way to Po's house in the early evening they were still there.

"I'd like to propose a toast," Max said, looking at Po and thinking how grateful he was that she emerged from this experience safe.

"A toast," came a chorus from the group.

"To the power and protection of strong friendships," he said. And they all drank.

CHAPTER 27

It was with a light heart that Po packed up her tote to meet the Queen Bees two weeks later. It seemed to her that the world was righted. So many loose ends had been tied down. Instead of walking around with her brain tangled into knots, she could see all the pieces of the puzzle and the pattern of what had before been just a mass of jumbled bits.

The day seemed to mirror her sense of peace, with the crisp, clean Autumn sunshine flooding every inch of the town she loved. "What a day," she thought with a happy sigh.

She found her friends gathered and waiting for her.

"I'm still celebrating that you're alright," Kate said, as she had every time she'd seen her in the last two weeks.

A chorus of "me, too" and "that's for sure," came right after.

"I'm fine," Po said with a smile. "None the worse for wear."

They all settled in at the table. Without a group project underway, they each brought whatever project they were working on. Susan was paper piecing a dramatic pinwheel pattern in blues and whites on the machine. Phoebe was working on a baby quilt for a friend. And Po had brought the small cat quilt she'd made as a token of their last project—and the latest in her collection of quilted memories—to finish the binding. The same job she'd done on the full-sized version.

"I never did hear who bought our quilt," she said.

"Oh," Maggie exclaimed. "It was Adele. Isn't that wonderful? She was by far the highest bidder, and she was so excited to have it."

"And the Humane Society was pretty pleased, too," said Eleanor with a smile. "It was one of the most valuable items they auctioned."

"How much did they earn, total?" Selma asked,

"It was more than $10,000," Eleanor said.

"I've been wondering what ever happened to Fitzgerald and the other dogs," Phoebe said.

"I heard that they weren't keeping the dogs," Kate said. "After all, Jack Francis was pressuring Angela to kill Fitzgerald."

"That dog boarding facility will be wasted space with no dogs, for sure," Po said.

"I think they've found new owners for all the dogs," Maggie said. "Other devoted breeders and showers."

"And I heard that the proceeds from the sale went to Mercedes' estate," Po said. Who had indeed heard that. From Max, who was in the know.

"Just so they'll all be with people who will really care for them," Phoebe said.

"Is Jack Francis recovering from the shock of being accused of murder?" Selma asked in the lull that followed.

"He was cleared right away when Angela was arrested," Kate said. "But I don't know about the dealership."

Leah laughed. "It sounds like Melanie has stepped up on that front," she said. "Maybe she was cowed by her mother all those years. But not any more. She inherited the bulk of the estate and moved right into the power vacuum, I think. I heard she's turning things upside down."

"Well," said Eleanor. "If the relationship survives it, maybe that was the answer all along. It could be a great partnership. Jack Francis' quick talking and a little leavening and business smarts from his wife."

"I just can't be nice about Jack Francis," rejoined Phoebe. "Even if it turned out that he wasn't the worst of the bad guys here, he still conspired with Angela to steal Fitzgerald, didn't he?"

"Could be," Po admitted. "I sure think so. But I'm not sure the police are pursuing that part of the investigation any longer."

"After the trouble it caused to have Fitzgerald disappear?!" Phoebe was appalled. She turned to Maggie. "They sure weren't going to let you off the hook if it was your fault that he was gone."

"True enough," Maggie said. "But since it wasn't my fault, I'm happy to have the whole thing settled."

"Mercedes didn't cut Jarrod off, did she? After all that she bullied him, it seems like he's due," Phoebe said.

Po decided not to share all she suspected about Jarrod's friendship with Helen. No need to complicate his life at this point. He'd be the target of irrepressible gossip in Crestwood for at least 10 years without her help. So it was Leah who answered.

"I think he got something," she said. "But he's moved out of the compound, I think. So maybe that was part of the deal; Melanie got the house."

"What a horrible time that family has been through," said Po, thinking back.

"Even suspecting that Mercedes had been murdered couldn't really have prepared them for the reality," Susan agreed. "And to find her body at the dump. It seems so terrible."

"P.J. said it was a first as far as they knew, using a body bag for a Great Dane to hide a murder victim. Poor Mercedes was probably picked up from the freezer just a few hours before they came and searched the clinic," Maggie said. "And here I told them it was just impossible that she'd been murdered in my treatment area." She looked around, as if asking for understanding. "I really just couldn't imagine it."

"How could you?" soothed Po. "None of us could."

"We went over all the drug logs with a fine-toothed comb.

She had altered them in places, but it was tough to catch. I think she'd also been selling drugs, siphoning off a tiny amount from each vial to sell, and filling it back up with water. I feel terrible."

"Well, it's not like you escaped unscathed either," Kate said. "How much did you find so far?"

"We're still trying to track it all, but we're up to at least $8,000 that she stole from the practice for this year alone," Maggie said. "No wonder we weren't making what I expected."

"How is that possible?" Phoebe asked, shaking her head in disbelief. "It seems like such a huge amount."

"Well, one thing she did was pocket the money if somebody paid in cash," Maggie said. "She had also opened an account with a name that was almost exactly the same as one of my suppliers. And she wrote herself checks to that account. When I reviewed my bills, it looked fine."

"Wow," said Phoebe, big-eyed. "That is seriously sneaky. Imagine if she put those powers to work for good."

Maggie laughed. "Yeah, imagine," she said. And then she sobered again. "I sure made a lot of mistakes," she said. "I thought Angela was such a godsend. I never once suspected."

"Max said that's how it normally goes," Po said. "He says small businesses get stolen from all the time, and never realize. And he says it's so often the person you'd least expect. That great employee you couldn't live without who comes in early and leaves late and never goes on vacation. That's partly so they're there to cover their tracks."

"Well, I guess I can take comfort in the fact that I'm not

alone," Maggie said. "I sure fell right into that trap. She seemed to care about the success of the clinic. I was always impressed with how well she did with clients. And she just loved the pets, I thought. And then she stole Fitzgerald. Imagine…"

"You know I should have put two and two together," Susan said suddenly. "Remember that day you came by the store, Po? I was going to walk the river that night? Well, I did. And I didn't see the dog, of course. But I did see Angela drive by. I assumed she'd been out looking for the dog, just like I was. But now I bet she had him penned out there somewhere." Susan looked discouraged. "I walked the other way, figuring she'd checked in that direction. If I'd checked up on her, I might have found him."

"Trust me," Po said. "I think we all had opportunities to put two and two together that we missed. It was tough to get the bits to square up."

Kate laughed. "Always the quilter, Po."

Po looked at her and smiled, happy that they all could laugh again. Happy that the cloud had lifted from her town, and her dear friend Maggie's face.

"It will take time for everything to feel back to normal," Maggie said, as if she were reading Po's mind. "But I finally feel certain that we'll get there."

"Yes," Po said. "We'll get there. And faster than you think, I bet."

When she got home, Po ironed the new binding on her cat quilt. Taking down the summertime piece she had hanging in the entryway, she hung it up and admired it. The four cats expressed all the personality she'd hoped.

At her feet, Hoover seemed to be admiring the new piece also, and he suddenly woofed twice in apparent satisfaction.

"I quite agree," Po said, leaning down to scratch his ear in his favorite spot. "What a memory. What an experience. What a wonderful group of dear friends."

Acknowledgements

First, I must thank the Persian Pickles for bringing the joy of quilting to my life and inspiring me both to sew and write. You are my very own Queen Bees.

Of course, very special thanks to Sally Goldenbaum, creator of the Queen Bees and my writing mentor. I appreciate your support during the whole of the writing process and your generosity in sharing the Queen Bees with me. How could I be so lucky to have the perfect friend arrive in my life? It's a blessing to know such an incredible writer and all-around wonderful person.

Additional thanks go to my friends and advisors and teachers and supporters in the veterinary field. They deserve all the credit for the details I got right and none of the blame if I got anything about the workings of veterinary practice wrong. I feel privileged to work with veterinarians; as a group you are caring and generous with your time and your ideas, and as individuals you're even more terrific.

Thank you to my dad for being my early reader and providing such valuable feedback. And finally, hearty thanks to all the family and friends who cheerfully supported me during the writing process.

Marnette Falley

About the Author

Marnette Falley is a proud member of the Persian Pickles, which meets in Lawrence, Kan. She is an editor at a veterinary publishing company and lives in Bonner Springs, Kan., with her husband, Joe, her 10-year-old daughter, and two adoring dogs.